Endorse  *right hand*

"The Rwanda genocide is referred to again and again as an example of the viciousness and inhumanity we humans are capable of. It is also often pointed out that this was "Christian-on-Christian" violence. However, that word "Christian" was first coined in the ancient Roman port city of Antioch and it referred to "those who are Christ-like". So the Rwanda tragedy serves to throw light upon the limits of religious systems, no matter what label that system bears. It also brings to light the contrasting story of those whose aim was, and is, to be Christ-like.

Immaculée's story is a thread of hope amongst the many whose thin veneer of religion gave way to inhuman acts. God promises in the Bible that He will walk with those who love Him and seek, whole-heartedly, to do His will. In fact, He promises to work for good "to those who love Him and are called according to his purposes" in all circumstances, no matter how horrific they might be. The Bible makes it clear that mankind was created in God's image for good, but generations of rebellion and selfishness have warped people almost beyond recognition. Nevertheless, God's grace is still available to redeem the most wicked and He is the protector of those who call on His name in faith. This story illustrates the depths to which human beings can sink, but also God's faithfulness to His people."

Lynn Green. *YWAM*

"I've always loved hearing the worlds big stories told from the perspective of the ordinary by-stander, the person caught up in World news and history defining moments but who has desires, hopes, fears and dreams that I can relate to even though my own life have been lived half a world away. In one sense Immaculée's story is one of those, it captures in easy to-read language the beauty and innocence of a land thrown through ugly times by the un- resolved every-day resentments and jealousies that get passed on and grow generation-to-generation. But in another sense it is not, because Immaculée is certainly not an ordinary by-stander. C.S Lewis once observed that forgiveness is such a simple idea until you really have something to forgive. That Immaculée found forgiveness and even reconciliation with those that murdered and tortured her family and friends is genuinely remarkable. Her story both inspires me and it challenges me, to let go of my rights to justice for the sake of my own and a greater good too."

Christen Forster, Christian Teacher and Author of the 'Supranatural Life' and 'Jesus Centred Bible' series' of books."

Under His Mighty Hand

A Story of Faith and Overcoming from the Rwandan Genocide

The Story of Immaculée Hedden
As told to Richard Hedden

All Scripture quotations are from the Holy Bible, Today's New International Version (TNIV) © 2001, 2005 by the International Bible Society

ISBN 978-1-291-86967-5

Cover designed by Paulo Carvalho

Cover Photo of the Blue Bathroom Wall at Gisimba Orphanage by kind permission of Kresta King Cutcher, 2005.

Cover photo of Richard and Immaculée by Nice Bowers.

The map of Rwanda was the creation of Dane Wood

Email contact of Richard & Immaculée:rhedden2@gmail.com

Contents

Acknowledgements

Without the help and kindness of so many, the writing of this book would not have been possible.

For their support, encouragement and grace whilst we completed the work on the book, thanks to the YWAM community at Harpenden.

For their editorial and technical support thanks to: Claudia Chaigne, Umar Turaki, Jenny Lowen, Colin Forbes, Penny Weightman, Sue Pratt, Dane Woods, Ina Steyn, Sosthene Maletoungou and Lauren Nelson.

Thanks also to those who have given so much moral and prayer support, especially David & Elisabeth Cross, and Ingrid & David Coombes.

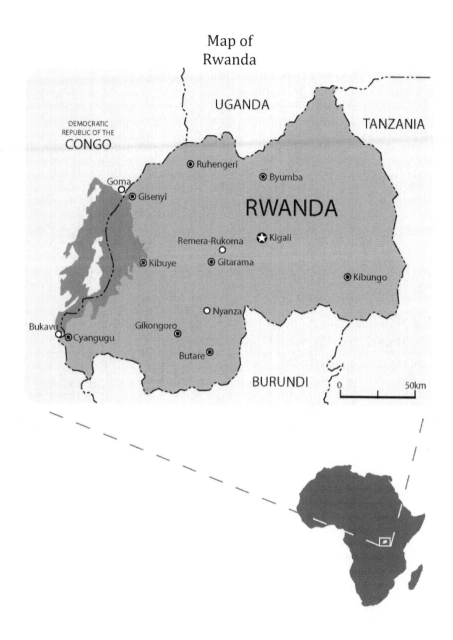

Map of
Rwanda

FOREWORD

The 1994 Rwandan Genocide against Tutsis, which claimed an estimated 1,000,000 lives, still marks the world as one of the greatest atrocious mass slaughters of the 20th Century. Rwanda in 1994 was a land of unimaginable horror, bloodshed, fear and tremendous pain. One cannot forget to note the inhumanity that was evident in the perpetrators and the hopelessness of the victims of the Genocide.

This was a time when most Rwandans asked the same question, "Where is God?" The centuries old Rwandan adage, "God spends the day elsewhere and returns to Rwanda to spend the evening and night" was seemingly untrue. Thousands were massacred in churches while praying and calling Him to save them whilst others were given to the mass slaughter as if fed to the dogs by their own friends and neighbours. To the human mind, it is hard to imagine that the God of love and mercy was in Rwanda in that period; nevertheless, through accounts like Immaculée Hedden's, one can truly attest that God was in Rwanda for each single day of the 100-day Genocide.

Under His Mighty Hand is a book that will impart faith to your life in inconceivable times. Immaculée Hedden beautifully shares with us her journey of faith and trust in God's voice. As you will read the candid and deep recounts of Immaculée's testimony, you will find that there were more times than one that the sting of death was ready to sting her, however, she made the decision to position her faith on the invisible God for help and salvation, even in the most dire of times.

Perhaps you may need a financial breakthrough, a family reconciliation, a healing of a particular disease, a solution to a long-term problem that you have had or any other issue that Immaculée's story has not directly addressed: have faith. Even as small as a mustard seed, the Bible says that it can move a mountain and throw it in the sea.

For Genocide survivors and others going through difficult times of life, I highly recommend this book, hoping that as you read it, you will find your faith in God restored and encouraged that our Lord is there in your situation and ready to save you. I personally know the long journey where Immaculée walked, from the genocide's nightmare to now. God has done a tremendous work of healing in her life! Why not you?

Apostle Dr Paul M Gitwaza

The President and Founder of Authentic Word Ministries and Zion Temple Celebration Centre, Kigali, Rwanda

PREFACE

Having been close to death, I know how fragile life is. We are, all of us, one step away from eternity. I have lost many of my friends and loved ones because of the tragedy known around the world as the Rwandan genocide of 1994. My being alive does not make their loss any easier to bear. It does not make their faith any less real or significant. There are some questions to which we will never know the answer on this side of eternity.

I was born into the Tutsi ethnic group of Rwanda. Although I don't like to be called Tutsi, I am happy to be called Rwandan. The use of identity cards - stating a person's tribe - was introduced by the Belgians. Before that we were three groups, Twa, Hutu, Tutsi living together. Rwanda is a unique country in Africa. We have these three groups but no geographical division for each group and we all share the same land, language and culture. This is not found in other African nations, except Burundi. Intermarriage has caused a blurring of the divisions between the groups.

The Twa make up no more than one percent of Rwandan population and their origins were as the hunter-gatherers in the land. The Tutsi have always been a minority group in the nation, making up between 10 and 20 percent of the population at varying times in history. The majority have always been Hutu, being over eighty percent of the population.

Because our land, language and culture unite us as a nation, I prefer to be known as a Rwandan. The heart cry of so many Rwandans is to be known and accepted without the questioning and curiosity as to which tribe we are and what happened to us. Those things are important, but we want them to come in the context of genuine relationship.

Going back a number of centuries the Kingdom of Rwanda was ruled as a monarchy, with the king always succeeding from one or two clans of the Tutsis. This status quo changed around 1959 to1962, when the monarchy was overthrown and a republic established with a Hutu president. This republic was maintained for just over thirty years. Tutsis were largely excluded from the nation's public and political life. Time came when a group of Tutsis - mostly exiles in Uganda - challenged this exclusion and sought to be re-integrated back into the life of the nation.

The government line hardened and exclusion was maintained. Inside the country there was mass propaganda and the creation and perpetuation of myths about Tutsi - that the Tutsi were going to make Hutus slaves; and that Tutsi were not Rwandan at all but outsiders and should be sent back to Ethiopia where they came from.

Rather than move on from the past through forgiveness and co-operation, the leadership at that time chose the route of clinging to power and genocide. This had devastating consequences for all Rwandans.

The international community were also part of the problem, who during colonisation, brought in ideas of hierarchy of race and classified groups in the nation. Then later on, when the genocide happened, the wider international community all but abandoned Rwanda in her hour of need.

The mixture of these forces, both within the nation and outside it, resulted in a massacre of Tutsi and anybody who opposed the plan to wipe them out. This included many Hutu who desired to build a nation of inclusion and many who stood up to the killing by protecting Tutsi or refusing to participate in the bloodshed.

There is a legacy of survivors because of the bravery of so many Rwandans and a handful of Westerners who resisted the regime of the killers. Spend a moment to consider the legacy of those who were able to make a difference but held back or turned away.

Before the genocide, God spoke to a group of us in the church that many needed to get prepared to go to be with Him. For them, it was time to "go home;" their work on this earth was finished. God is the one who knows best for each one of us. It seemed that He was saying it would be better for some of us to "go home" than to stay alive during the difficult time coming. The faith of many would be tested and it would be difficult for some to remain faithful during the days ahead and they might give up. When we prayed this is what we felt God saying.

God spoke specifically that He would preserve my life. He put His words in my mouth so that I could encourage others. I know that He kept me alive, because He has more for me to do. I stayed

Under His Mighty Hand so that you may know something of the mystery of His love.

His love is a mystery. It is not that we do not know His love; the mystery is that we do not know it completely. There is always more to discover.

Does God love those who were killed in the genocide? Yes, indeed He does. Does He love the killers? Yes, indeed He does. He loves those as much as He love those killed. Does God love the survivors, like me? Yes, indeed. He loves all of us and I am still trying to understand His love. I remind myself that we are in a fallen world and this may even lead us to choose to kill each other. May you also know His Mighty Hand in your life. May these words of mine reach your heart. May they point you to Jesus of Nazareth: the mighty redeemer, liberator, friend, healer, provider, ruler, and the one who gives joy to our hearts.

My intention is that this book first and foremost gives glory to God and tells of His goodness: it is a testimony. For those who want to read the history of the genocide there are many good books to find in the *Further Reading* section at the back.

My loving husband, Richard, has written my story from what I have told him and he has tried to preserve my voice throughout. In places where my broken English or poor grammar has come through I hope that you can hear first of all the heart of the testimony I want to share.

Despite my desire to give glory to God through this book, I am all too painfully aware that it comes out of tragedy. In a country which had a population of about eight million, estimates of one million lives were lost in approximately one hundred days. This happened in a nation which is barely bigger than Wales or the state of Maryland. Rwanda is 26,338 km or 10,169 miles square and can easily be traversed in a day.

Each loss of life was a tragedy and a bereavement for the families affected. There are some people who are the only surviving members of their family. Even as I told my story through this writing I came to see my own need for grieving the passing of loved ones, including my Dad, for whom I had not had time to really grieve before.

The Rwandan Genocide raises many questions: Why the loss, the hatred, brutality and coercion? Even as I find out about the Nazi regime in Germany and other wars in the Balkans and elsewhere, I see that these are age-old problems of humanity. This is a fallen and needy world. It's the same old story, the same question it raises in my mind – when will we grow up into the original design God created us to be? When will we live as one people, serving one another and respecting each other? When will we grow up to celebrate our differences, not being fearful of the other, not exploiting weaknesses or living out of pride? When will we all celebrate those parts of the whole we call Rwanda- the Twa, the Hutu, and the Tutsi. *Oh Father God, when will we grow up into the men and women you created us to be?* That is my prayer.

CHAPTER ONE

History – Rwanda's and Mine

Rwanda – the land of a thousand hills, known as 'the tropical Switzerland of Africa', is my motherland and the country that I love. The many beautiful hills and valleys, mountains and lakes make it shine as a jewel in God's creation.

When I was growing up, I remember seeing impala and gazelle jumping in the grass near to where we lived. At night we would hear laughter like people, only to realise they were hyenas cackling. It was funny how they sounded so much like humans. Neighbours sometimes would say they had seen leopards in the nearby forest and they warned us children not to go there on our own. My uncle told me that when he was young, lions would occasionally come and kill cattle at night.

One afternoon when I came home after playing with my cousin next door, I entered our house and heard the noise of what sounded like a hyena. It made me afraid and I ran back to my cousin's house. When we both came back to see what was inside, I found my uncle having his afternoon nap, snoring very loudly!

Sometimes during the day, we used to go into the forest nearby to pick fruit from the trees. Monkeys would jump up in the branches from one tree to another and when we threw fruit up to them, they would catch and eat them. After they had finished eating they would throw the stones of the fruits back to us. It was as if they were playing a game with us.

I used to see so many different kinds of birds. Grey-crowned cranes, tall and elegant, seemed to dance in the sunshine as they moved around in a flock.

In the morning when the sun rose, giving brightness, it told of the new day coming. Then at midday I would see my shadow in the middle of my legs, telling me that it was noon. Rwanda is very near to the equator and so the sun is always overhead at noon.

Sunset would bring a festival of colours. The last hour of daylight brought a myriad of shades of green in the hillsides. Behind them the distant hills were a pale blue and above them the pink of the sky. There is so much beauty for the eye to behold in Rwanda.

I spent so many evenings sitting outside chatting and laughing together with friends and family. When it was full moon, the moonshine made you think it was day. Often I would look at the night sky and see countless stars. Many times we would go from one house to another, sharing testimonies and praising God. During those days I never thought things would change. I never thought life would change - from the light of the moon, the sunshine, people's kindness and loving one another, to killing.

*   *   *   *   *   *   *

Before Rwanda became independent from Belgian colonial rule it was a monarchy led by the king. When the king died someone from the Royal Family took over, one king after the other, not unlike other monarchies. There were only one or two clans from which the king came. There was some colonisation: the Germans first came in 1894 but then they fell in 1916; the Belgians then came in and stayed until 1962. Each one of those people brought their own ideas. The Belgians introduced the idea of identity cards in 1926 and in a way this brought some division among us as Rwandans. I don't know if they knew that what they were doing would bring such a huge division in my country, as it happened.

Between 1959 and 1961 there were big changes in Rwandan society; that's when the revolution happened. When the Belgians came they were ruling with the Tutsi and then they switched to rule through the Hutu. The revolution started in 1959 when they started killing and that was the time when so many Tutsi went into exile. This happened many times until 1973 when the Hutu President Habyarimana took the government in Rwanda. Even after that there were some people who went into exile in neighbouring countries because of one reason or the other. So in Rwanda there had been several times of crisis of genocide, not just in 1994.

It was among those exiles that I had so many relatives, including my biological parents. They went to Congo, some others went to Uganda. Mum and Dad settled in a place called Bibwe in the zone of Masisi in North Kivu Province which borders Rwanda. This was the place where the UN put all of the refugees escaping from Rwanda to Congo at that time.

*   *   *   *   *   *   *

My parents had one child after the other in quick succession. I'm from a large family of eight girls and one boy. Two of my sisters passed away when they were young and one died in a car accident in Nairobi. So we were left five girls and one boy.

It happened that my brother, Eugène, was born eleven months after me. When I was still a baby, it was decided that an aunt and uncle who lived in Rwanda would look after me and I was given to them. In the Rwandan culture it is not unusual for extended family to take in children to spread the burden of family life.

When I was still very young, my aunt became sick and passed away, leaving my uncle to look after me. I don't even remember how my aunt looked as I was too little to recognise her by the time she died. Later on their son got married and because of our age difference he was able to take me into his family to look after me. So, for most of my childhood it was he and his wife who brought me up. They became like parents to me. They had children of their own – six daughters – and they became like sisters to me. Their names were: Florence, Claudine, Claudette, Theophile, Angeolette, and Rita.

For years I had no discernment that this was not my real family. But one day, as I was walking along the street I heard some people say that I looked like my Mum. They wondered if my parents were still alive. There I was living in a family and quite naturally I thought I belong to them and yet when I went out, I heard people saying about me: "She really looks like her mother. Are her parents still alive?" To start with I thought they we talking about my aunt who passed away, but where we lived everyone knew that she had died. This made me start to wonder if there was another family that I had. When I saw some people walking in the street, it made me wonder if I was related to them.

One day at school it became clear that I was not in my real family. We were asked to say which family we were from and I had to bring my identity card to show my teacher. When he saw it he said, "No that's not your real family. That's not your real father or even your clan. I know who your father is. His name is Mwunvaneza."

Despite the confusion in my mind, what the teacher said began to make one thing clearer to me. I used to hear my uncle and cousins talk about some people called Stephanie, Mwunvaneza, Eugenie, Lea, Bona, Eugène and Jemma. At that time I didn't know who they were talking about, but now I knew that they were my dad, my biological sisters and my brother.

After I found out that I had some other people who were my real family, I prayed asking God to show me my parents. God answered my prayer when my eldest sister, Lea, came in 1980 and took me to Congo. I was so excited at the prospect of being reunited with my parents.

When my sister Lea came for me, she did not know me nor I her. At the time we lived in a rural area called Busoro, between Nyanza and Butare in the south of the country. Lea arrived with a cousin, Hilary, who worked as a teacher in Nyanza.

As Lea entered the room, I stood up to embrace her and as we hugged, tears of joy swelled in my eyes. I had no memory of her as a baby, but she was my real, biological sister and it was special to be with her. Her complexion was light – African light-skinned – and she wore a lot of make-up. As we sat and talked, I couldn't stop the disappointment I felt in my heart. The Rwandan culture at that time said that those who put on make-up hadn't been raised in a good way; and my sister was one of those. It took me time to realise it wasn't to do with her being bad but simply because she had been brought up in a different culture to me.

After a few days we set out for Congo, first travelling to Gisenyi in the north-west and then crossing to the border town of Goma. My brother, Eugène, was studying in Goma and we visited him for a short while. From there we travelled on to my parents' place in Bibwe some 160 km from Goma.

We arrived at my parents' when it was early in the evening. I followed Lea into my father's house. The room was lit by a solitary kerosene lamp. There was no electricity in Bibwe or much further beyond. A quiet expectancy filled the room as Lea led me over to where my Mum and Dad were sitting.

"I have brought your daughter," Lea said.

As they rose from their seats, years of absence began to fall away and a well of laughter from deep within us broke out and mingled with tears of joy as we hugged each other.

*   *   *   *   *   *   *

A few days later, another sister, Jemma, arrived from Uganda where she lived with my grandmother. We were in the time of school holidays and the plan was that Lea, Jemma and I would go to Kisangani to visit another of my sisters, called Bona.

Bona had married young and her husband, Rugira-Jean, was a wealthy businessman. He came all the way from Kisangani to meet us and then took us to see Bona. We flew from Goma to Kisangani by plane. I remember when we walked through the airport terminal, some Congolese people said to us, "Banyarwanda, Banyarwanda!" which is the way to address Rwandan people. In a way they were jeering us for being outsiders, even though the Congolese president had decreed that we had a right to be citizens of the Congolese nation. But any sense of shame disappeared at the excitement of flying for the first time and then meeting up with Bona.

We had a joyful time as sisters together, talking for hours and sharing our different experiences. Kisangani is built on the river plain, and is a big port to the river Congo. They showed us the port and then upriver to the huge waterfalls. Kisangani was the most hot and humid place I had been to. I would take two showers every day to keep myself cool.

After our holiday there we flew back to Goma. Jemma went back to Uganda to continue her studies and I started to study in secondary school in Bibwe. The school was about three kilometres away and I walked there every day with my friends. The country was so green and beautiful. In April, during the rainy season, the paths would get muddy and we would slip and slide on our way. We had to pass through a mountainous place to get to the school and that was especially treacherous when it rained.

When the school holidays came I used to go back to Rwanda to visit. I travelled with other friends who were also Rwandan and had also come to Congo for their schooling. On our way travelling between Bibwe and Goma I would often see chimpanzees and gorillas by the side of the road. In some places there was dense forest and it was very lush and green. In other places there were big farms with their fields. It was a beautiful place in those days.

In my heart I was divided by having a family in Congo and a family in Rwanda, but it was all part of who I was growing up. Sometimes I felt I wanted to see my real parents, and sometimes I wanted to see the family who brought me up. When I came back to Rwanda in the holidays I realised I felt more at home in Rwanda. I hadn't spent most of my childhood with my real family and so Congo never felt like home.

I was never able to be open towards my Mum to ask her why some of us were scattered as children. My parents didn't tell me why I didn't live with them as a young child. Maybe they thought they would make me sad if I knew the truth.

I love all my sisters, but I'm especially thankful to Lea because she made effort to come to take me so that I could see the other members of my family. I respect her because she did that even though it wasn't easy for her. At that time if you were living in exile, to come to Rwanda you should hide yourself, otherwise they might put you in prison. I am so grateful to God for bringing her.

I stayed in Congo for three years studying. Then the teachers stopped working because they hadn't been paid for so long and I wasn't able to finish secondary school. So my secondary schooling was cut off and I wasn't able to complete it. I came back to Rwanda and went to a technical college to learn some practical skills, like sewing and social life. I then found a job for a while with one of my aunts. After this job finished I found other work in a dress-maker's shop called *Chez JoJo*, named after the owner.

I worked in JoJo's shop from 1988 selling fabric and doing the finishing work on dresses, adding sequins, beads or embroidery to the clothes. The shop was in the centre of Kigali and I lived nearby at a hostel for young people run by the Catholic Church called *Jeunesse Ouvrière Catholique*, we knew it simply as 'JOC'.

My life revolved around work and church. Most Tuesday and Friday evenings I was at choir practice. I loved being part of my choir which was called *Chorale La Fraternité* – this means Fraternity or brotherhood choir. We were made up from many different church denominations and, although we all lived in Kigali, came from all over Rwanda.

We came from different ethnic backgrounds, mainly Hutu and Tutsi, but we were open to having singers from the Twa and we also had a Congolese member. The only thing in common we had was being brothers and sisters together in Christ. We all had the same experience of being born-again by the spiritual renewal Jesus had given us. This gave us a special unity that only God could give us.

We were invited to various churches, schools and universities to give performances. We communicated the love of God through song, drama and preaching and teaching. The presence of God with us during these times always gave me joy. God gave me many friends because of His love amongst us.

On Saturdays I would always go to a Bible Study run by Scripture Union in a church nearby. These meetings also brought together people from many different backgrounds, but united by our hunger to study God's Word together.

Throughout the years I worked for JoJo she trusted me. When she was away on business or visiting her children, who lived in Belgium, I would often be the one in charge of receiving payments from customers. In the shop I loved to be surrounded by the diversity of colour of the different fabrics we sold.

JoJo had a good reputation for making clothes and many families came to the shop to buy for weddings, baptisms or other important occasions. Sometimes we had fashion shows where we would take many clothes designed by *Chez JoJo*. One time I went to the famous Milles Collines Hotel to help dress the fashion models with our clothes. Those occasions were a time of excitement as beautiful women and handsome men walked elegantly on the catwalk displaying the clothes we had designed.

Life was so busy for me during those years, but sometimes life was hard for someone from my ethnic group. I didn't do exactly what I wanted to do or finish secondary schooling in Rwanda. I was far away from my parents and couldn't go and see them whenever I wanted as it was difficult for me to travel. Even though I didn't study all I wanted to, God was faithful to provide me with work at *Chez JoJo* and so many friends to be with. In all things I am thankful to Him.

CHAPTER TWO

A Calm Word Before the Storm

The week before the genocide happened was the week before Easter. I took holiday to go to a Scripture Union conference about an hour's bus ride from Kigali. The venue was the secondary school in Remera-Rukoma, Gitarama district. I met many friends from different parts of the country and met new people who became my friends too. I loved being part of one big family of believers. We were mostly born-again believers and it was a joy to be together. We talked and laughed and prayed together. At the conference various speakers taught us from the Bible and brought us words from God.

Our times of worship were exuberant and joyful and we danced a lot, celebrating the wonder of our God. This year, however, mixed in with the joy, there were some serious words coming from some of the speakers. On Maundy Thursday we had a time of fasting and prayer. During the meeting some people spoke out words and impressions they sensed were from God. One person described a picture of blood flowing like river in the church. Another person shared a picture they saw of a person putting down their Bible and picking up a machete.

These pictures raised discussion amongst us. Some people didn't think that this could be real blood that would flow in the church. One lady said, "How can human blood flow in the church? This is the time of Easter and so maybe the blood flowing in the church is the blood of Jesus."

As daunting as it was to contemplate, many of us did think that God was speaking to us about the coming days when blood would flow in the nation of Rwanda. But the most disturbing thought was that it would flow in the Church. Wasn't this supposed to be a sanctuary, the House of God, a place of prayer for all nations, tribes and tongues?

News filtered through that some killings had taken place in Kigali. This was not good news to hear but the Conference leaders encouraged us not to be afraid. The country was going through a time of transition and a new power-sharing government was being organised. Tensions were running high in the nation. Even though there may well be trouble coming, the conference leaders encouraged us to guard our hearts from fear and hatred. We were told to be united in spirit and to be salt and light to the world. Even though fear breeds fear, we were to be a people of peace who could react in the opposite way. If we saw violence or if anything happened to us, we should love our enemy. We should bless those who persecute us as Jesus teaches. This way people would know we were different and not like the ungodly. We were to respond out of love. Difficult though these days were, we were learning to be more united as the people of God.

*   *   *   *   *   *   *

The conference ended the next day and as we dispersed to go back home, we hugged each other. As I embraced one of my friends, I said, "My friend, may God keep you safe." I looked up to the sky and saw the clouds gathering. It looked like rain was coming. It was April 1 and the month of rainy season had begun.

I had taken a holiday for a whole week and I planned to go for prayer and fasting at the Scripture Union Centre in Kigali. A group of four of us had agreed to go together, but one thing and another happened which meant that I went there alone.

We were not all from the same tribe, but because we were all born-again we didn't have any sense of exclusion because of our ethnicity. We were good friends without a thought for all the division and crisis going on in the nation. As we travelled back, Denise stopped off to visit a friend of hers and Pascasie went to visit her family near our conference venue. The other friend, Donata, had not gone to the conference because she went to visit her family in Bugesera, not far south of Kigali.

I sat in the taxi bus on the way back to Kigali watching villages pass me by and taking in the myriad shades of green in the hills and fields. As I pondered what to do I realised I still had a strong desire to fast and pray for my country. I decided to go to the Scripture Union Centre the following day even though I would be alone.

The Scripture Union Centre was quiet when I arrived. We had been together at the conference but now it was the Easter weekend so most of the staff were on holiday. I was shown a room where I could pray and I started the next day.

I prayed from Easter Sunday until the following Tuesday. I spent much time before the Lord worshipping and reading through the Bible.

As I read through chapter 51 of Isaiah, the part of the passage where it says that people will die like flies, jumped off the page at me. Somehow I felt that God was speaking to me that these events were going to happen in Rwanda, but it was beyond my understanding and I couldn't put it in my mind how this would happen. I moved on with my prayer time.

God also spoke to me through verses 7 and 8 (Isaiah 51) *"Hear me, you who know what is right, people who have taken my instruction to heart. Do not fear the reproach of mere mortals or be terrified by their insults. For the moth will eat them up like a garment; the worm will devour them like wool. But my righteousness will last forever, my salvation through all generations."*

The Lord continued to speak to me through verses 11 to 16 where it says:

> *"Those the Lord has rescued will return.*
> *They will enter Zion with singing;*
> *everlasting joy will crown their heads.*
> *Gladness and joy will overtake them,*
> *and sorrow and sighing will flee away.*

'I, even I, am he who comforts you.
Who are you that you fear mere
mortals,
human beings, who are but grass,
that you forget the Lord your Maker,
who stretched out the heavens
and laid the foundations of the earth,
that you live in constant terror every day
because of the wrath of the oppressor,
who is bent on destruction?

For where is the wrath of the oppressor?
The cowering prisoners will soon be
set free;
they will not die in their dungeon,
nor will they lack bread.
For I am the Lord your God,
who stirs up the sea so that its waves
roar-
the Lord Almighty is his name.
I have put my words in your mouth
and covered you with the shadow of
my hand-"

Those last words were really important to me: *I have put my words in your mouth and covered you with the shadow of my hand.* As I read them I heard an audible voice and I turned around to see who was speaking to me. The room was completely empty. *That truly was the voice of God*, I thought to myself. I had so many questions in my mind: *How and why would people die like flies?*

The day after finishing my time of prayer and fasting I travelled back home across Kigali. It was Wednesday 6 April. When I got back to my room, my roommate Françoise was not there. I found a note on the floor that had been pushed under the door. I picked up the piece of paper and sat on my bed to rest for a moment.

Glancing up, I looked at the picture on my wall. It showed a young boy holding in his arms a lamb. There was a scripture written on the picture saying: *"The Lord is my Shepherd, I shall not be in want" (Psalm 23:1)*. I used to put it in my bedroom wherever I moved to. Whenever I looked at my picture I thought about Father God who was holding me in His arms and that gave me security. Since I was born, He was the Heavenly Father who looked after me from one family to the other. Being brought up separately from my biological family, the Lord showed me that He was the one who looked after me more than anyone else.

I opened the note, and on it was a message saying my father had passed away on 2nd April. This was the same day that I had gone for my prayer and fasting. I sat on my bed and cried alone, but with Father God holding me in His arms, just as the boy was holding the lamb in my picture.

The light was fading and I had to leave as I had arranged to go to a cousin to break my fast. I changed my clothes and packed a small bag for the night. My plan was to come back the next day or the day after that, then unpack everything and get ready for my cousin's wedding the following Saturday. There were so many things going on and my feelings were mixed, because now I also had to decide whether or not I would try to get to my father's funeral in Congo, no matter how difficult this would be for me.

As I was leaving JOC, I met my friend Consolée, who was one of my best friends. I really loved her. She described to me what had been happening while we were away. She told me to be careful not to travel in the evening because a lot of killing had been happening recently. In some places people had already moved out because of the killings.

She said, "Be careful. Take a taxi quickly before it gets dark, so you too are not killed." We walked together up the hill towards the roundabout where I would catch my taxi. As I looked out across the hills of the city I was again struck by the beauty of my country. To hear of all the killings that had happened recently broke my heart and I couldn't help but wonder what would happen over the coming days. Would the violence pass over as it had done on previous occasions of unrest, or could something more serious be happening in this land of a thousand hills? Even though God had been speaking to me that people would die like flies I still couldn't imagine how this would happen and I hoped that the unrest would soon calm down.

"Immaculée, be careful where you go these days," she said. "Make sure you travel early and don't move around in the dark. Some people have already moved out of some areas of the city because of the recent killings. Things have been changing so quickly."

"Bye for now, my lovely friend," I said as we hugged before parting.

I hurried on up the hill and jumped into a taxi headed for my cousin's house in the south-west of the city. People in the taxi were not talking and there seemed to be an air of mistrust. Usually I love to talk to people wherever I am but now with this condition in the nation I was unsure who to talk to. I didn't know if I was sitting next to someone who may want to kill me.

CHAPTER THREE

At Hilary's Place

The taxi bus dropped me near Hilary's house. I walked over to their compound and knocked on their big iron gate. One of their house girls came to let me in. I greeted Hilary, her husband Bosco and their children. I was excited to see them all, especially because Hilary had a new-born baby girl, whom I hadn't yet seen. Hilary always used to say that she would like to have a baby girl; her other three children were boys. They gave their baby the name, Mutoni, which means "cherish" and she was for all of us an excitement. Once again, however, my feelings were mixed because I was carrying the sadness of the death of my father. When I arrived there, they asked how I was and I told them that my Dad passed away. They stood and hugged me awhile.

Hilary said, "So sorry to hear the news, Immaculée, that's so sad."

"How did you get the news?" Bosco asked, "Your family are in Congo."

I told them how I found the note on my bedroom floor as we moved over to the dining table to have a meal together.

In a way I did not know how I felt, there were so many question marks for me. Of course there was the grief that my father passed away, and it was a double sadness because I was wondering if I would be able to go the funeral. It was very sad because it was dangerous for me as a Tutsi to travel through the north of Rwanda to Gisenyi. People had already been killed on the road simply because they were Tutsi or came from the south of Rwanda. Despite the difficulties and dangers, I talked with Hilary about how to try and get there. We talked about how it wasn't an easy journey to make, and I would need to trust God for protection.

*   *   *   *   *   *   *

My mind went back to the last time I saw my father. It was 1990 and he was very sick with rheumatism. I had taken one month's holiday from my job at JoJo's to travel to Bibwe to visit my parents. There wasn't a lot of traffic travelling there from Rwanda. In fact there were never any taxi buses going there, only two Land Rovers that ever travelled down that road from Goma – one was from the monastery and another for a businessman who went there.

When I arrived at Goma that time in February 1990, I had a very, very hard time to find transport to Bibwe. I had to wait for almost three weeks then finally I found a lorry going in the right direction. It was not going all the way to Bibwe though and I got a lift part of the way to a junction 25 kilometres from Goma. Later that night, another lorry going towards Bibwe came. There was no room in the cabin though and so I had to ride in the back. It was a lorry for taking food and it was also full of ladies from the local Congolese villages. I didn't know what they were talking about because they were chatting in their language whilst they sat there with their baskets. As we drove through the mountains in the evening it became windy and we were shaken around in the back of the truck.

Being shaken around in the lorry was a frightening experience for me. It brought me heartache to think of all the hardship of getting to see my parents. I prayed to God in my heart: *I don't know what you can do to bring back my parents to Rwanda but anything that is necessary please do it.*

When I arrived at a place called Mweso, 100 km from Goma and 56 km from my parent's place, I couldn't find another vehicle to take me the rest of the way. Fortunately I had a friend who lived in that town; their parents had been neighbours of ours when they lived in Bibwe. So they were able to host me. After three days of seeing no vehicle to give me a lift, I went into the Catholic Church and started praying. I prayed to God to see if I would have a car to continue my journey. That was the first time that I saw a vision whilst I was praying. In my vision I saw a car! So as I came back from my prayer I had assurance from God that I would get there to see my parents even if for only one day.

I talked to my friend and said, "I think I will go because I saw a Land Rover car."

She asked, "How did you see it?"

I said, "As I was praying and I saw it in a vision. It was red."

Then sure enough, after two days, a red Land Rover came and was able to take me to Bibwe. Unfortunately it had to come back the next day and my time of holiday had already finished. So I did see my Daddy that night, but I didn't have time to visit any neighbours because it was already night by the time I arrived.

As my Mum was accompanying me in the morning so I could take the same car to come back, I was very upset. I looked at my Mum and her friend, who happened to be the mother of the friend I stayed with at Muweso, and I asked her, "Mum would you like to come back to Rwanda? Do you think one day God will bring you back to Rwanda? Would you like to go back if you can?"

Mum just laughed at me and said, "No, no, no, we have already become Congolese." Although I was determined in my prayer to see my parents come back to Rwanda, it seemed in her heart she did not have any hope. Later on that year, in October 1990, a group of Rwandan exiles in Uganda invaded the north of Rwanda and started a civil war. Although I wasn't part of it, I'm sure that those who were fighting against the Government were doing so because of the injustice of not being able to return to their country. These exiles were mainly Tutsi and were called the Rwandan Patriotic Front (RPF).

I tried to fight back the discouragement I felt as I hugged my Mum goodbye and then got in the vehicle to travel back to Rwanda. It was the last time to see my Dad and the memories of that time were part of what I felt in my heart when I found out about his death. In a way I couldn't grieve. I don't even know where they buried him, because nobody we know lives there now. I hope maybe he will be in heaven, because he was a very good Christian in the Catholic Church. I remember when I lived with him for three years he used to pray morning and evening before we slept. My sister, Laetitia, told me that before he passed away he was behaving in a very good way, so perhaps I will see him in heaven; because only God knows where He put him.

*   *   *   *   *   *   *

With all these memories churning in my mind, I finished my meal. We went to sit in the living room and I was able to share the joy of cuddling Hilary's newborn baby. As I was holding Mutoni, it was something special for me. God had given Hilary something from her heart's desire: a very beautiful baby girl, her firstborn girl.

It came time to go to sleep and I was shown to the guest room. I slept soundly that night, but dreamed that there was war going on. In my dream there were some soldiers who wanted to kill us and I was hiding in a house.

In the morning we heard big news on the radio. Last night the president had been killed in a plane crash. He was returning from Tanzania in his private jet and as it was coming in to land, it was shot down and crashed into the presidential garden just next to the airport. Some people were happy that the president had died, but for most of us, we knew the serious consequences of his death. Two years ago the president of Burundi had been killed and many Tutsis died afterwards as a result. Now with the Hutu president in Rwanda having been killed we feared the worst for Tutsis in our country.

That morning a cousin telephoned us to tell us that some of our relatives had already been killed. This struck terror in our hearts; furthermore, we could hear gunfire and screams around us. So much killing had started so soon after the news of President Habyarimana's death. Bosco tried to go out and get some money from the bank but it was closed. We tried to send the house girls to the market but it was closed. The Government had set up roadblocks making it difficult to get about.

On the radio it was being broadcast that no one should leave their house for security reasons. On the hate radio - Radio-Télévision Libres des Mille Collines - it was being broadcast that those cockroaches and their spies must be killed because they had killed the president. This was their code language and the signal to kill Tutsis, who they called cockroaches. For me now it was impossible to go outside and move about freely.

Soon after the genocide started, and we began to hear that relatives around us had died; the words that God had spoken in my time of prayer and fasting started to make sense to me. People were dying like flies around me as the word says in Isaiah 51:6. So much of the killing was being carried out by the Interahamwe and the Presidential Guards. The Interahamwe were the youth militia of those politicians determined to carry out the genocide.

Another thing that began to make sense was the way God was leading me to comfort people around me. Sometime later, I took time to pray and ask God's word for everyone. Then when we met in the evening to pray, I shared the words of encouragement God gave me for the people.

On another occasion I wrote scripture verses that God gave to me on pieces of paper. I prayed and then asked everyone to pick up every verse and read them. I waited till last and picked the remaining paper. As I read mine, it spoke to my heart and confirmed what God had spoken to me at the Scripture Union Centre, in Isaiah 41:10 where it says:

> *"So do not fear, for I am with you;*
> *do not be dismayed, for I am your*
> *God.*
> *I will strengthen you and help you;*
> *I will uphold you with my righteous*
> *right hand."*

*   *   *   *   *   *   *

My cousin's house was surrounded by a wall, so from outside people couldn't see into the house or the garden or anywhere in the compound. In a way this had become my hiding place. If nobody came inside you could feel safe from the evil going on all around. It was not easy to stay in one place though. We didn't have the freedom to go wherever we wanted, even though the house was spacious. In our bedroom, as girls, we could stay there and feel quite comfortable. Some days we would spend some time sitting outside within the compound.

Life was just about surviving and there wasn't enough food. My cousin used to have a store of food, but the genocide started before they had bought supplies and so there was not very much in the store. So we had to start reducing the size of our meals from very early on. We used to eat just in the evening, and even then eat very little. Then it came to the time that everything finished. We would have drinking water when it rained. There was the time when we didn't even have tea to drink.

At the beginning of May the local councillor, Grégoire Nyilimanzi, came to Bosco's home. He checked the identity of all of us, especially we who hadn't been there before. When he saw my identity he said to Bosco, "They don't want this tribe." This was difficult for Bosco because the authorities had made it clear that if you hide Tutsi then you may be killed also. So Bosco was in danger because of me and probably because of his wife, Hilary.

A couple of days later, on May 3, some soldiers came to search the house and we all had to go outside. They checked all of our identity cards. Hilary's and mine showed we were Tutsi, but Bosco and his sister showed they were Hutu.

In Rwanda at that time, because of the injustices that had been happening towards Tutsi, some people changed their ID card to Hutu. This enabled them to find a better life by gaining access to education and work. Bosco's father had done this and so now he and his sister held Hutu ID cards despite being Tutsi.

As we were all standing outside, Bosco was telling them, "This is my sister and these are my children."

Seeing the family resemblance they said, "Eh...you can see it."

Bosco then turned to me and said, "And she is our guest."

Because they had seen my ID card, they said, "You will be surprised." By this they meant that they would be back to kill me because of my Tutsi identity.

"And this is my wife," Bosco said to them.

Again they said to her, "You will be surprised."

The soldiers left the compound and immediately afterwards Bosco left to go to the roadblock. Time passed and he still didn't return. Then at about three in the afternoon a good friend of his came with a soldier who said he was a sergeant of the battalion of Mount Kigali nearby. The friend's name was Abdul and he stayed waiting for Bosco to return. We sent Mukunzi, their first-born, to try to find Bosco, but he came back saying he didn't see his father at the roadblock. They sent him to another roadblock to see if he was there but again he came back without having found him.

Then Abdul talked to Hilary about the reason he had come. He said that on May 7 there was a plan to do a lot of killing. The Interahamwe were going to "clean" as they put it. The idea behind the big massacre would be to remember the death of Habyarimana one month ago. Abdul wanted to bring some soldiers to protect Bosco's family on that day. He felt some kind of loyalty to Bosco because of his kindness to him. Abdul was a car mechanic and had fixed Bosco's vehicle in the past. Once when he was in hospital, Bosco had looked after him well in his time of need. He brought him food and visited him many times.

It was nearly six o'clock and beginning to get dark. Suddenly some men came through the gate – Interahamwe militiamen. One stood at the window with his gun pointing through, another banged at the door. I was sitting down holding Mutoni and so I stood up to let them in. When I opened the door the militia immediately looked in the living room and saw the sergeant sitting on the sofa. So without giving me attention they went over to the sergeant and one spoke to him, "I would like to see your ID card."

The light was fading and with no electricity to work the lights, he asked me for a torch to read with. I said, "We don't have a torch, but we have a lamp that we charged when the electricity was still there. Can I give you that?"

He said, "No, no," and pulled out a tiny torch from his pocket. He peered down at the ID card using the torch and saw that this guy was a sergeant from the government army. Then he said to him, "I'm sorry. We are just at work."

The sergeant said, "That's fine."

Then the four militiamen left and Abdul continued talking to Hilary. A little while later he left with the sergeant.

Bosco still didn't return and we began to be anxious that something had happened to him. He didn't come back for a jacket or anything to eat. We went to bed that night fearing the worst.

Very early the next morning, before it was light, some people from the neighbourhood came into the compound and broke into the house. They started stealing things we had like radio and TV. Other things they put in the guest room and locked the door, taking the key with them.

They spoke to Hilary, "Why are you just sitting at home, why don't you go to bury your husband?"

This broke the news to us that Bosco had been killed. From our neighbours this was extremely cruel. They too had become part of the Interahamwe and it was heartbreaking to see. They continued to speak to us in an intimidating way, focused on stealing, and then left.

In a way it was so hard to grieve. Because of all the killing going on around we thought to ourselves: *When will be our time to die too?*

I wished that Abdul would have come before Bosco was killed. We don't know God's mystery, we only know what we see, but we don't know what we don't see. Abdul came when he had found someone from the government army to accompany him and talk about protecting all of us together, but Bosco had already gone. God had changed the killers' plans through bringing the government soldier and confusing them but it was too late for Bosco.

*   *   *   *   *   *   *

After the death of Bosco, life became much more difficult. We never went outside the house and tried to make sure we were always out of view. When the militia knocked on the gate, we always ran away and hid in the garage.

During those days I used to say to myself: *Oh God, when will I be able to go out again? When will I be able to go to the church again? When will I see the sun again?*

We just hid ourselves and rarely risked opening the curtain. When we did we saw the bright sunshine, but still we were afraid, because there was a lot of bombing going on. So, though inside the wall gave us safety, we remained hidden in the house so the bombing and gunfire did not hit any of us.

Sometimes when I thought about the desperate situation and heard bad news I wondered if I would survive, but so many times I had hope. I always had something to speak.

I remember Hilary saying that she dreamt about all kinds of violence also happening to me. I said to her, "This will not happen to me, in the name of Jesus." In my times of prayer I said to Jesus: *When I was able to give you glory, I didn't do adultery or all those things. This is the time to glorify your name and to honour me. I may die, but I will not be raped, in the name of Jesus.*

During those days, when the genocide dragged on and we had no way of knowing how long it would continue or what would be the end. I said, "Surely if God has created us, there will be some people who survive, because no man's plan will prosper. No man can completely destroy a tribe, if it is God who made us; surely some people are going to survive."

I spoke to God in prayer: *I don't want to die because of being born a Tutsi. If I die for being a Christian, then that was my choice, but I did not make a choice about which tribe or country to be born into. If being a Tutsi is a mistake, then that is your mistake not mine. But it is you who created me so you should protect me.*

When the houseboy of Bosco's cousin came to Hilary's house once, he said "This place is like heaven. Nothing that happened to us has happened here. I wish everyone could come here." He paused and then continued, "Ah, probably they will come later. It can't stop here, I am sure they will come here. They will do all kinds of bad things also here to you."

"They may kill me, but I believe that God is going to keep me from all kinds of things like raping," I said.

"Well everyone at our house was also Christian," he replied. "Everyone was praying there too. Why do you think it will not happen to you?"

I said, "When Jesus was going to heal people he said: 'Let it be as you believe.' So I believe by faith that nobody is going to rape me." Then the houseboy left.

Everyday life was difficult. Even though we didn't have much food we managed to eat a very small meal in the evening. There was a time though when even that food ran out and we didn't have anything to eat. But at least God always provided us with water. I remember even when the water wasn't coming through the taps, God sent rain and we collected the runoff in every container we had. We then had water to drink and wash with. I prayed for God to provide water and we always had it, either when it rained or when the taps suddenly started running again.

It came to the point when my nephews believed that because I was praying for water, I could pray for electricity and it would come. They said, "Immaculée, you can even touch the light switch and the electricity will come."

I said, "It doesn't work like that! It's not me who brings anything. It's by the grace of God, when we call on His name. Jesus can do that, but it's not me." I wanted them to know that it was God and not me who was providing for us.

*   *   *   *   *   *   *

One day, later in May, a soldier came into the compound and looked around. The government had ordered that the gates of everybody's houses should be left open to allow the militias free access to all the houses, but we had decided that we would keep ours closed. When this man found the gate closed, he shook it violently. He kept shaking it and when he realised he couldn't open it, he jumped over the wall.

He looked around the compound and happened to spot me through the window. When he saw me he ordered me to come outside. "What are you doing in there?" he shouted. "Come outside and I will finish your life right now!"

"I'm reading my Bible." I said, "Peace be with you."

I picked up my identity document and went outside. Louise, one of Hilary's house-girls, was already outside and she stood there watching what was going to happen. She was a Hutu and so was not in the same danger as I was.

I handed the man my identity document and waited for him to inspect it. I knew this could be my last hour, but I stood firm with my eyes fixed on the soldier and prayed silently in my heart: *Lord, if this is my time to come to you, receive my spirit. But if it is not, then I rebuke the evil spirit at work in this man so that he will not touch me, in Jesus' name.* He looked at my identity document, which clearly stated that I was a Tutsi, and then looked me up and down. He then looked at my identity document once more and gave it back to me. He walked away from me towards the gate and left the compound.

"Immaculée, how are you feeling now?" Louise exclaimed to me, "That guy was ready to kill you. Did you realise that? Maybe you don't know when the gun is ready to fire, but I know. It's a miracle what happened."

"Well, I wasn't afraid." I said, "I was thinking about the God who protected Daniel in the lion's den and who enabled David to kill Goliath. So I wasn't afraid."

The name of Jesus had protected me. A friend of mine had taught me how to rebuke demons without speaking aloud and this was what I did. Once more I knew that I was under the mighty hand of God. It was remarkable the way that the soldier gave me back my identity card. In Rwandan culture you show respect to a person by giving them something with two hands. That is how he gave me back my identity document. The soldier went from commanding me to come outside, so he could finish my life, to showing me respect!

CHAPTER FOUR

Moving to Gisimba

Hilary's three older children moved after Bosco died. They went to stay at an orphanage nearby, called Gisimba Memorial Centre. We knew it as Gisimba Orphanage. An aunt of ours, called Triphine, worked as a social worker there. She wrote encouraging Hilary to go there as well. Triphine feared for Hilary's life. There was more protection at the orphanage, she explained in her letter. There they could be together and, if it came to the worst, die together.

Hilary told me she was going to the orphanage to see about evacuating to there and she would let me know her decision when she got back. When she arrived there she realised that conditions there were much worse than she had imagined. People were overcrowded and there was no water for washing baby Mutoni.

When she got back she said, "I'm not going there, I'm going to stay. Death is death wherever it happens, and I want to stay here where there is some comfort and space, even though we don't have food and so many other things we need."

Two weeks later the militia came to the house of Bosco's cousin, who were our neighbours, and killed the whole family. The houseboy of that family who had visited us previously saying "we were in heaven" came with the news. He told us how they had been killed in a very bad way, including their baby who the Interahamwe threw in the toilet.

Hilary realised that our turn would probably be next and she made up her mind to go back to the orphanage. As we talked things over she said, "I may be killed there at the orphanage but the situation here is now more serious than I had thought. They might come to find us and even throw us down the toilet after killing us." She asked me to decide what I should do.

I went to my bedroom and lay on my bed staring at the ceiling and pondered what to do. The soft mattress beneath me was a small comfort in the midst of such a terrible situation. Yes, there was space in Hilary's house but it was no longer the safe refuge it had been. Yes, it was not smelly like the orphanage but we needed to move somewhere soon to have any chance of surviving.

I thought about two friends of mine who lived in the same neighbourhood. Samuel and Alice were their names. They were Hutus and newly married, and they were my best friends from my church. Early in May, Samuel had come to see how I was and we had a chat. He told me that many people from the choir where we used to sing had been killed.

I told him about a dream I had about one of our friends, Joselyne, with whom we used to sing. I had no idea about whether she was still alive or not, but in the dream she was in a beautiful place. She was with a crowd of people and they all wore white robes. They looked joyful and were singing. In that place was a peaceful light, bright and yet soft, not harsh like the sun which burns the eyes. This light you want to keep looking at because it is so calm and warm. Among the crowd I didn't recognise anyone else, only her. I think God wanted to tell me that she had gone. She was special to me and always used to call me her daughter.

Samuel said, "I'm amazed, because God has shown you that she is in heaven. She is in the best place where you saw her in that dream."

It was hard to hear the news from Samuel that she had passed away, but I had the assurance that I would see her again in heaven.

Before he left that day, Samuel gave me one hundred Rwandan francs. It was not a lot of money, but it was meaningful for me, showing me that they were still my close friends and standing with me in the midst of what was happening. In that time people couldn't know who was still their friend because many were betrayed. That is why Samuel's visit and gift were so precious to me. I gave the money to Hilary and it contributed towards buying something to eat.

As I thought about where to move to, my heart was with my friends Samuel and Alice and I planned to go to their house. Even though they lived in the same neighbourhood, it would be a difficult journey to get there because I would need to avoid the roadblocks guarded by the Interahamwe. It wouldn't be easy to reach there, but my thinking was that I would be safe as soon as I got there. I looked forward to having time with them, being able to talk and pray together.

Before I slept that night, I prayed to God to make it clear to me if this was where I should go. Only He knew my right path.

That night God did answer my prayer in a dream. In the dream, I was going to their house and then on the roadblock God showed me that I had been caught and all kinds of terrible things was happening to me ending in death. It was a horrific dream. I knew that God was warning me and that gave me assurance and some measure of comfort.

When I woke the next morning I didn't need to pray further. I knew I had to go to the orphanage with Hilary.

Gisimba Orphanage was only a few hundred metres away from Hilary's house. However, to reach it we would need to pass two roadblocks guarded by the Interahamwe. The situation was extremely dangerous; I needed God's protection now more than ever.

*   *   *   *   *   *   *

As we were getting ready to go to Gisimba Orphanage the next day, Hilary spoke to me, "Remember that we are not going together, in case they may kill us. If we go separately, one of us at least might get a chance to survive."

She continued, "I will put the malaria medicine next to the telephone for you to take." Her plan was that I would pretend to have malaria, which would provide me with the need to go to the orphanage to get an injection from the nurse there. If I was stopped by anyone on the way, that's the story I would tell them.

I didn't respond to what she said because that was her way to try and help me. I prayed and spoke to God: *I know the cupboard where the medicine is stored. I can go and take it any time. I might be killed tomorrow and I don't want to die after having just sinned by telling a lie. I can't help you by telling lies but I need your hand of protection. I pray that if it is your will that I don't go with the medicine, then let her forget to put the medicine next to the telephone as she has planned.*

The next morning, Hilary got up one hour before me at about half-past four, and then she left the house. After she had gone, I got myself ready to go. When I looked over towards the phone I couldn't see any medicine. I moved over closer and could see she had not put it there. *That's great!* I thought, *God doesn't want me to take medicine.* In a small way it was an assurance that God was with me.

I dressed myself and stuffed my night clothes and a spare dress under the dress that I wore. With my Bible, a small devotional book and my identity card I left the house.

Louise, the house girl, said, "I will be your company and see what happens." Being a Hutu she could move outside and pass freely through roadblocks and checkpoints.

I opened the red-rust coloured front gate and Louise followed me. We walked down the slope of the driveway and onto the road. As I turned right I could see the roadblock no more than twenty meters ahead of me. There were a number of large stones on the red-dust road to prevent any vehicles from passing. For me the problem was not these large stones but the two men that sat there next to them, guarding the roadblock. These men were Interahamwe, the ones who attack together.

As I walked toward them I chatted with Louise, trying to make us look busy. I could not hide myself though. Even when we had left the compound moments earlier, the men must have been aware of movement going on. Now as we approached them and passed behind them they turned around to look at me.

I continued to talk with Louise and as I passed them, I saw the expression on these guy's faces. Their eyebrows rose, nearly jumping to top of their foreheads. They looked surprised, shocked and somehow frightened. Rather than get up and arrest me as they were supposed to do, they remained sitting and didn't even ask me anything.

We walked on. What an amazing God we have! He is the defender of the weak and I wondered what was happening around us in the spiritual realms.

After we had passed, Louise said, "Oh, Immaculée this is a miracle! I had better go back now, but may God who helped you here help you at the next roadblock. I don't know if you will get through that one, because it is very strong, and they don't allow people to pass without stopping them. You don't live in this place and so it will be more difficult for you to pass through."

I turned up a path that passed between two houses and up to the road that would take me to the orphanage. On the path the words of 2 Kings 6:16-17 came to my mind: *'Don't be afraid, those who are with us are more than those who are with them.' And Elisha prayed, 'Open his eyes, Lord, so that he may see.' Then the Lord opened the servant's eyes, and he looked and saw the hills full of horses and chariots of fire all around Elisha.'* Although I could not see them with my eyes, I sensed that there were angels protecting me. Those who were with me were more than those carrying out evil around me.

As I walked up the path there was a loud explosion. The ground shook and I fell to the ground by instinct to protect myself. As I was picking myself up I peered to the end of the path where it joined the road. I could make out people running along the road. As I got closer I could see there were some soldiers and Interahamwe militia. They were running with their guns and machetes and other weapons they had. I waited a little longer for them all to go past me. They were running in the opposite direction of the orphanage.

I stepped out into the road and peered down towards the orphanage. The heavy roadblock that I had heard about was there, but there was nobody guarding it. The guys running in the opposite direction had abandoned it. So, I walked on and came to the roadblock. There was still smoke rising in the market place next to it where the mortar had exploded from the fighting. I kept on walking, thinking about those chariots of fire all around Elisha, and praising God. After a few hundred meters I reached the orphanage.

And so I passed through that place walking elegantly! When I arrived at Gisimba Orphanage they welcomed me. The God in whom I trust - the God of Abraham, Isaac and Jacob - He was with me. He is mighty to save, a great warrior!

CHAPTER FIVE

At Gisimba Orphanage

When I came in to the orphanage, I was met by my aunty Triphine. She said, "Look Immaculée is coming! Come in." She spoke in a tender voice. "I wonder how you walked through all the roadblocks." She knew that I was going to try and come because Hilary had already come. I greeted her with a hug and she showed me where I would be staying. I stood and looked across the dormitory where I was being put. It was full of people, absolutely crammed full. There were many children and teenagers and a few old women who had taken refuge there. We all had to share the same meagre space. The smell from the crowding was not good at all, with all of the windows closed and no fresh air coming in. Everyone looked very thin as did I by this stage too. Most of the children looked like they were suffering from malnutrition. Their swollen cheeks and feet told of the kwashiorkor disease that had begun to set in. The skin on their faces was lighter than normal, another sign of malnutrition.

I was in the girl's dorm and the other dorm was for the boys. In my dorm were all the smallest children, boys and girls together, and a few women. There were other rooms outside the main dormitory area and Hilary was staying with Triphine in the room where the pharmacy was. There was one toilet for our dormitory and because there was hardly any water for washing, the sanitary condition was very poor.

Many people had mattresses which they were sharing, about three people to one bed, but as for me I had to sleep on the blue sheeting provided by the UN. Because we could not wash our clothes or bedding, they became infested with fleas. I was fortunate in that I did not come to the crowded orphanage until June 2, about eight weeks after the start of the genocide. I had taken my night dress with me from Hilary's house, so at least I could change my clothes at night. The other ladies would sit close to one another, helping each other to kill fleas and take them out of their hair. As they crushed fleas with their nails they said, "We have life, but how long will we have to live like this?" But I thank God because for the whole time I was there I slept soundly; God gave me that blessing.

When I had arrived I showed them my identity card and they registered me as they had registered everyone staying there. For this reason we knew that there were about 475 people at the orphanage - a completely overcrowded situation.

Supplies were brought to us by a white missionary working for ADRA, the Adventist Development and Relief Agency. Water came in enormous barrels, loaded onto a truck and brought by the missionary. Whenever he was able he brought supplies of biscuits, tinned food and whatever else was available. He was very courageous to have done this for us. The most intense fighting between the government and RPF was going on around us. He could have been killed at any time because of the bombs exploding. Sometimes he couldn't get through because of the fighting.

The orphanage staff continued to serve us, despite all the difficulties. They made porridge, which we ate once a day. I spent almost one hour eating my porridge in a very small cup, because I had to take away a lot of hard bits. It seemed to me that it was probably animal's porridge and I made sure I threw the bits away rather than eat them! Sometimes we also had biscuits that had been brought for the children. There was very little water for drinking and I was always thirsty.

A few days into my stay at the orphanage, the landlady of my friends Samuel and Alice came to visit. When I asked how they were, the lady said, "Oh, didn't you know? Samuel and Alice have already gone to Gikongoro." They had gone to the place where Samuel comes from in the south of the country. I remembered the dream that I had before moving from Hilary's when God warned me not to go to Sam and Alice's house. I realised that God was showing me they were not there and that I would have died if I tried to go to their house. I thanked God again for His faithfulness and care for me.

The orphanage manager was a man named Damas Gisimba. A kind-hearted and compassionate man, he had risked his life by taking in so many refugees. He taught the children to respect each other, no matter what tribe they were from. He told them anyone who betrayed another to the Interahamwe would be shown the door and asked to leave the orphanage.

He saved two ladies from a nearby mass grave. These women were with us in the dorm and had difficulty moving. They had severe back pain, and some of the other ladies would give them massages to help ease the pain. I heard how Damas Gisimba had courageously rescued them after hearing their cries for help. He sent someone to tell them to keep quiet so the Interahamwe would not hear them, then late that same evening he went back and pulled them out of the pit with ropes. Sadly, the baby of one of the ladies was crushed to death in the pit, but through the courage of Damas Gisimba and the treatment of the carers, the ladies were alive and recovering. Although they still struggled to walk straight, their wounds were healing.

He really did try to care for and provide for everyone who came to him for protection. He used the money the orphanage had to buy food, then the money he had for himself, and then he asked everyone staying for any money they had to contribute to be able to buy food. He often sent some of the orphans to buy food supplies. He did this because people in the neighbourhood knew them already and they did not arouse suspicion.

When the militiamen suspected "their enemy" to be hiding out in the orphanage, Damas would not let them enter. One time he stopped us being massacred by his quick thinking and courage. Many Interahamwe descended on the orphanage with all kinds of weapons, knives and guns. They asked him to bring everyone outside. In defiance he stood at the dormitory entrance and spread his arms out saying, "You cannot come in. If you want to enter here, you will have to kill me first and then who will look after your orphans?" He never seemed to have any fear to confront the Interahamwe; in fact, they respected him.

Damas Gisimba's father had established the orphanage, and was well-known in the local community for all the kind work he had done for the people. The name of the orphanage came from the memory of his father; that's why it was called the Gisimba Memorial Centre. Before the genocide, almost all the children were from the Hutu tribe; so during the genocide the militia called these children their own. This created a dilemma for them when Damas Gisimba said they would have to kill him before entering the orphanage.

On June 12, Damas Gisimba came back into the orphanage distraught. Our relative, Triphine, had been killed by the Interahamwe. He had gone after them but had arrived too late to do anything to save her. They had tricked her into believing there was an injured person who needed attending to, and had lured her away to shoot her. The killers came back for her children, but Damas Gisimba begged them to leave them alone and they left.

I remembered the hug that Triphine had given me when I entered the orphanage and the tender way she spoke. If I knew that hug was the last one I would give her, I would have taken time to appreciate her and express my gratitude for all that she had done for me. How special she was to us. If she was not there, I probably would not have been able to stay at the orphanage. Many times she sent messages to Hilary encouraging us not to stay at home because of all the killing happening around us.

She suffered so much. I remember many times militia came to Triphine with wounds they had picked up while fighting with the RPF. She would help them dress and bind the wounds. Then they said to her, "OK, you are doing that for us now, but one day or the other we will come and kill you. Do it, but we know that you are all cockroaches. We have killed your husband, we will kill you too one day."

I'm sure some people will have a reward in heaven. Some people have suffered more than others. That's how I would describe the suffering of Triphine. Imagine having to put your hand on someone's wound and then hear them say, "You are binding my wound, but I will kill you later." And she kept doing it for the Interahamwe. She had extreme courage. We were very sad and mourned for her. That evening, Josine, her daughter, cried the whole night. We all cried the whole night. We said to each other, "We are losing her, we are losing her, and she has suffered so much." May God give her peaceful rest.

Toward the end of June, the Interahamwe threatened Damas Gisimba's life. One evening he came into the dormitory very upset, his eyes all bloodshot and said, "Don't fear death, death is all around. Fear dying without honour." The reason he was so upset was because one refugee had betrayed people hiding in the roof to the Interahamwe. Three refugees had been killed by the Interahmawe and this now put Damas in extreme danger because the militiamen knew that he had been concealing Tutsis in the orphanage. After that, we didn't see him in the orphanage again and assumed he escaped to take refuge for his life. We feared that he might have been killed but had no way of knowing. His younger brother, Jean-Françoise, was there, though, and took over as manager.

We continued to survive: eating little, drinking little, just hiding. Even through these hardships, my testimony is that God was sustaining us. We were inside and had shelter. It was the rainy season so we did not have the misery of trying to survive in the bush. We were not outside having to see so much death and killing. This was the hiding place God had given us. As I was sitting in the dorm I was grateful to God. I thought about the reality of God's word, that He would not test me more than I could bear. He was making a way for us; this was my deep conviction.

Those days at the end of June were days of extreme hardship. No supplies of food or water were getting through and there was heavy fighting going on. There were a lot of bombs exploding nearby and the sound of gunfire was deafening.

We had a time when, for three days, we had no food or water. People all around were desperate and they lamented because of starvation and dehydration. I tried to encourage them saying, "We need to give thanks to God. He has taken care of us till now. He deserves our praise. We mustn't lament because we don't know what God is doing." Deep down inside of me I knew that God was doing something for us, even though we had suffered so much hardship. I was reading the story of Israel in the books of Moses and Joshua. I could see how much they were led by God. Many times God came at the last minute when they called upon His name. Although God always intervened and performed miracles for them, many times they complained and sinned against God by their unbelief. They grumbled to Moses and said, "Why did you take us out of Egypt?" I could see that we were in a similar situation, we had seen God's faithfulness to make a way for us, yet most of us were grumbling.

After those three days, the man from ADRA came and brought us water and food. But even more than just bringing us food, he also came at exactly the right time. That was the day Damas Gisimba left the orphanage and many militiamen came to the orphanage. They intended to get us out of the orphanage so that they could kill us. When the missionary arrived he saw what was going to happen, he stayed as long as he could and his presence seemed to discourage the militia and they gave up their attempt to come in that day.

Who knows, if he had come earlier, we may have had water, but he would not have been there when the militia came. God brought him at exactly the right time, when we were in need of protection.

CHAPTER SIX

The Great Escape

On July 1, many people at the orphanage thought it would be their last day. At mid-morning a major from the government army came to the orphanage. Along with his assistant he talked to the young brother of Damas Gisimba, Jean-Francoise. They asked us to start dressing the young children in preparation for them to be evacuated. As they continued talking, people went over to the window because we could hear voices of people outside. The two women whom Damas Gisimba had rescued from the mass grave started shaking violently. Through the window they had seen those who had tried to kill them and this sent them into high trauma. They shook with fear and covered their faces with a scarf to hide themselves from those same militiamen. Everyone was afraid because we all knew that the orphans were our shield of protection and that as soon as they had gone the killers would come in to do their massacre.

I looked around me. Many people were shaking uncontrollably from the thought of imminent death. The children were still being dressed in preparation to go out. Was this finally our turn to meet death at the hands of the Interahamwe? There appeared to be no hope for us now.

The assistant went outside with Jean-Francoise, but the major stayed behind with us. Then he turned to us and said, "OK, listen to what I say carefully, this is very important. In five minutes, everybody must be in the bus. Run very quickly because they might shoot at you." We all knew that the militia had surrounded the whole building.

"Don't take any of your possessions," he continued, "If you live you might have things again, but the important thing is your life right now. I'm warning you if anybody is still here after five minutes, then your life is at the mercy of the Interahamwe."

What was going on? Were we being given a way out or was this just a trap? Everything was happening so quickly and I realised we had no choice to make. But I thought that maybe God was giving us a way out through this man. We got up and started to run. In spite of three months of hiding and near-starvation, people found energy they never knew they had. Even those two ladies who had injuries in their backs somehow found the strength to stand upright and run.

As I came out from the entrance of the orphanage I did not know what to expect. Would we be met by shooting? Would we all be gunned down? As we ran we saw many militiamen from the Interahamwe, heavily armed and with their guns pointing toward us. We continued to run out from the orphanage to the tarmac road where the coaches had been parked. I expected to hear gunfire at any moment but none came. What was happening? Why no shooting? Again I looked over to the militia and I saw the looks of dismay on their faces as some of the refugees who had been hiding appeared before their eyes.

"Look!" they said. "Look there is Pie and Isaac. They are alive – we thought they were dead!" Instead of shooting, they threw their guns down in anger, slamming them to the ground.

"I'm telling you, you have never killed a Tutsi!" One of the militiamen said out of frustration.

We made it to the coaches and clambered on board. Somehow we all squeezed into just two coaches. The coaches then moved off under the escort of the major. We were waved through the roadblocks and the terror of the militias guarding them. We heard the Interahamwe saying, "We will go after them so we will know where they are going. We can kill them later on. This is our city." And they did follow us in cars.

From Nyamirembo we drove into the city centre and arrived at the Catholic Cathedral, called Saint Michel. Government soldiers, and some UN, were on guard and we unloaded from the coaches. I heard cheering and looked over to see the face of Damas Gisimba! He was surrounded by children who were joyful to be with their 'father' again and know that he was still alive.

We were taken to the basement under the cathedral where there were already a lot of people, mainly children. It was being used to house another orphanage and we were to join them. The basement room was dark but at the end of the room, windows let in some daylight. The windows had mostly been covered in blankets though, preventing anyone from looking in and giving some protection in case an exploding bomb sent shattering glass into the room.

I reflected on the events of the day and marvelled how God had made a way for us. To me, coming out of the orphanage to the coaches had been like the Israelites going through the Red Sea when God did a miracle for them to escape from the Egyptians. It didn't make sense to me any other way. Why would the Interahamwe militia come in such great numbers from all over the city if they didn't intend to finish us off that day? That's how I saw it.

Although we had escaped from Gisimba Orphanage, we were still not free to be open to one another and express our thoughts. We didn't know what would happen, whether the Interahamwe would still win, because they said they would come back to get us. We didn't know what it might cost us to share openly with each other as we couldn't be sure of the background of everyone that was there.

The people who had caused the Interahamwe to throw their weapons in fury had been completely hidden in a separate room from us in the orphanage. One was Isaac, the husband of my aunty Triphine. Although still grieved by the loss of my aunt, I was glad to know that the father of their children was still alive. Another was Pie Mugabo, one of the leaders of Parti Libéral, an opposition party targeted by the extremists. He had been highly sought after by the killers and in fact the hate radio - Radio-Télévision Libres des Mille Collines - had already broadcast that he had been killed. This was one reason the militia had been so furious and perplexed when we left the orphanage. The killers used to make those kinds of mistakes, boasting that they had killed people, but God used their mistakes because they stopped searching for those people. In this case, too, He brought confusion among them because they discovered these men still alive.

The other group of orphans in the basement with us were cared for by an elderly European man with a long white beard. We crowded into this one large room under the cathedral, over 600 of us. The blankets we had to use were so full of fleas, it was disgusting. We were given some porridge oats to sustain us. The next day we heard more gunfire and the sound of bombs exploding. We could not be sure of our fate and whether or not the Interahamwe might still get in to cause a massacre.

There was rumour that the Interahamwe were planning a big massacre on July 5, and this would be the commemoration of the former President Habayarimana taking power in Rwanda on that day in 1973.

By the evening of July 3, however, the noise from the fighting began to die down. When I woke up the next morning it was quiet outside. Everyone wondered why it was so quiet. The window was covered by the blanket to make the room much darker. Some people near the window opened the blanket a bit. People were calling each other to look outside the window. I was curious to go over and look outside as well. It was still before sunrise, but as I looked over toward the national bank I could see a soldier. He was wearing a different uniform from the government soldiers. He was a little bit thin, but he was standing firm. The strap of his gun was looped over his shoulder and the barrel pointed toward the ground.

"Something must have happened," people around me said. Until then we didn't know whether this would be good news for us or not. It was still an uncertain situation.

"Maybe these are the inkotanyi," someone said. Inkotanyi was the name given to the RPF. Quietness continued into the morning. It was a strange feeling after the intensity of the bombing and gunfire we had been used to. Later on, word got through that Kigali had fallen to the RPF and they were trying to secure the city for us. Maybe this was it; maybe this was the liberation we were longing for. But we were still cautious, waiting to see if it was really true.

As more time passed, the quietness and calm outside continued. Excitement was breaking out among everyone in the basement. It seemed our liberation was real: liberation from the génocidaires. People around me started dancing.

CHAPTER SEVEN

Life After Death

I sat in the gloomy light of the cathedral basement to the side of the room watching people dance. Hilary was on the other side of the room in the corner. One lady came over to me and said, "Immaculée, why are you not excited? The RPF have captured the city. Why are you not standing up and dancing? We're delivered!"

"How can I dance? How can I stand up and think about dancing?" It was time for me to think about the people whom I had lost, people I loved. It wasn't long before we were evacuated that Triphine was killed.

I said, "It's a shame, it's a shame, because she would have survived with us."

Hilary survived, but her lovely husband was already killed. Bosco had always been kind to me. I remembered times we used to chat and make jokes together. I really missed him. Hilary's parents were killed. Her two sisters, their husbands, and children were killed. At that time we didn't know about the ones who had survived. There was no way of knowing. So I thought: *We survived, but we lost so many people. We lost many of our relatives, we lost all of our friends; we've lost many people. So what does it actually mean to survive?*

In the afternoon I saw a cousin of mine, Gaspard. Excited to see him alive I got up and ran to give him a hug. I couldn't believe that he was alive. As a journalist he worked in Butare in the south of Rwanda. I thought he had already been killed but he told me how he had been able to escape south to Burundi with his family. He had come back with a Swiss journalist who wanted pictures of survivors in the city.

A couple of days later I saw another cousin who was a soldier in the RPF and this made me think that the genocide was really over. It was so good for me to see some relatives and for news to filter through about others who had survived.

Now we were able to talk more freely without fear that what we said might be used against us in betrayal. Triphine's husband, Isaac, spoke about the tiny room he had stayed in for nearly three months. On the day we were evacuated, he explained how the Interahamwe had asked what was inside the room and Jean-Françoise told them it was used for storing medicine and the French people had gone back to their country and taken the key.

Throughout that time they didn't leave the room once. At night Damas Gisimba would come and give them food and keep them informed about the war. If there was any risk of them being seen through the window in the door someone would tap on it to warn them. The six of them hiding would then all cram into the small bathroom, within the room, and keep silent until the all-clear was given. Hearing this story filled my heart once again with gratitude for Damas Gisimba's courage to protect us from the killers.

A lady spoke about what happened to her on the day we were evacuated. When we had already arrived at Saint Michel, some Interahamwe had started separating some adults from the children, saying there was not enough room for everyone to stay here. They loaded her onto a pick-up truck with some others and started to drive it away, but the white missionary from ADRA stopped them and brought it back for fear that they were being led away to be killed. No doubt this is what would have happened if they had been given the chance.

One day I went back to my room at JOC hostel to see what had happened there. The room had been looted. Clothes, money, and the two sewing machines I owned had gone. Those two sewing machines were brand new; one electric, one pedal. My heart was sad that my things had gone. I had hoped that God would somehow protect them, but I even had a dream that all my things had gone, so what I saw made sense to me. What I did have still was my life, unlike so many of my good friends who had perished.

As I stood there in my room, I noticed that not everything I owned was missing: the picture of the boy holding a lamb was there on the wall. It hung in the same place, untouched, my assurance that Father God was still holding me in His arms.

My roommate, Françoise, had been killed on April 7; the day after the plane had come down. I thought about what would have been my fate if I had not gone to Hilary's. Denise and Donata, whom I had planned to go for prayer with at the Scripture Union centre had been killed too.

My lovely friend Consolée who had walked with me to the roundabout on my way to Hilary's had also been killed. If I knew it was my last time to see her, perhaps I would have taken her with me; perhaps God would have protected us both. I remember as she hugged me, she said to me, "Bye for now." But the bye-for-now has become bye-forever. I will see her in heaven where there is no death.

*   *   *   *   *   *   *

We stayed at Saint Michel for about three weeks. The RPF were able to bring us some food which they had taken from abandoned shops. They brought milk and rice and instructed us to stay and wait until they knew that the part of the city we were going to was secured. They could not be sure all the Interahamwe militias had already gone. At that time the militias were still killing innocent people where they could.

I heard that on July 4 the RPF had surrounded the whole of Kigali and then gave the government army and the Interahamwe militia a way to leave the city through the main exit routes via Mount Kigali and Nyabarogo to the west of the city. They then went towards the Congolese border and went into exile with thousands and thousands of others. Even though the strategy of the RPF had been to give the government forces a way out, they still needed to search the city for militiamen hiding out in houses.

In those days it was hard to resist temptation and my faith was tested. I found evil was as strong after the genocide as during it. During the genocide every kind of evil was happening, especially killing, but after the genocide, evil changed strategy and tried to destroy my soul. People started to go out and loot shops and homes. Once Isaac saw me standing in Saint Michel when people were about to go. He said to me, "Come on Immaculée, you've got to go and find some clothes too. This is not sin. After all they have taken all our stuff. Even the Israelites went to plunder the enemy's things after their victories."

In a way people were justifying what they were doing. From my perspective I couldn't do that, because I would have felt guilty. In my heart I thought: *I have been preaching to people. It will be a shame to see me going to loot. I am sure if Jesus was here he would not go to loot anything. I want to walk in the opposite way and trust God to provide for me without stealing. There are so many people who have passed away, and what good is their stuff to them now? I have life and I will wait on the Lord for His provision of new possessions.*

This was now an opportunity for me to live out the teachings of Jesus. I fought hard to die to the desire to go and steal things. It wasn't easy, but I didn't want to lose the intimacy of His mighty hand on my life. That was what was at stake for me.

I was sitting at Saint Michel and then people started appearing, bringing things back from the city centre. I saw the clothes they were carrying and exclaimed, "Wow, I can't believe it. These clothes were from JoJo's shop where I used to work. See, that blouse was from the fashion show we had in March! How did you get in the shop? Was anything left there? Look, all this material is from the shop. I remember it very well. I can't believe that there were still things in there. Didn't the Interahamwe loot it before?"

They said, "No, no, they didn't loot. In that area the Interahamwe were keeping watch." One of the nearby shops was owned by the brother of Habyarimana's wife and so nobody went to steal in that area during the genocide.

The next day I went to see JoJo's shop for myself, it's not far from Saint Michel Cathedral. I was not sure if it was safe to go in to the city centre on my own, so I checked with RPF soldiers I met on the way and they said it was okay to go through.

When I arrived, I saw that they had broken the window and it was easy to enter that way. I checked the back of the shop where the tailors used to work and found the door still locked. Nearly all the material had gone. I wrote a notice to put on the shop front which read: "This shop has been taken back by the owner. Do not enter."

*   *   *   *   *   *   *

In my attempt to behave in a godly way, it got to the point that some thought I was stupid. It all happened because of Bosco's brother-in-law, Vincent, who used to come to visit us at Hilary's home during the genocide. He came to find us at Saint Michel and he asked me to stay with him. Sometimes when he came to Hilary's house during the genocide he spoke to me in a mocking way. One day he told me, "Go to the roadblock where they are killing everyone, if you really trust God, and I will see if you will come back. I will see if you will really trust God."

I said to him, "I can't go because you said, or because I want to see if I will be protected. If God says go, I am sure that God will protect me, but what you say is not part of believing in God."

For me, in a way, he was testing me. I thought it was similar to when Satan tested Jesus and said: *Jump to see if you are the Son of God...it is written that the angels will help you (adapted from Matt 4:6).*

When Vincent found us at Saint Michel, I could see that he was struggling with fear. He had been a soldier in the government army in the past but now worked as a watchman at the home of someone from the Belgian Embassy. He carried a gun during the genocide but was now afraid that if the RPF heard about this they would question him and arrest him on suspicion of being part of the genocide. He spoke to Hilary about me going to stay with him for a while to show that he had been protecting people. Hilary told him to ask me about that, but she was really expecting me to refuse because of the way that he had been mocking me during the genocide.

When he asked me, I thought a while and then I decided that I would go with him. I wanted to respond in the opposite way. So I said, "It's okay, we can go."

Hilary didn't understand me, she said, "Why should you do that, when you remember what he said to you?"

Part of my decision to go was because of Jesus' words: *Love your enemies and pray for those who persecute you, that you may be children of your Father in heaven (Matt 5:44-45). Bless those who persecute you (Romans 12:14).* So I went, even though people around me couldn't understand my decision. I reacted the way God told me to in the Bible, not according to the way Vincent had treated me.

The house of the Belgian worker, where Vincent was watchman, was just a few minutes' walk from Saint Michel. I went there along with Vincent's sister-in-law, Vestine, since I didn't want to go there alone as a woman. The Belgian was not there, no doubt evacuated at the beginning of the genocide along with so many other expatriates, but Vincent continued to keep watch over his property.

We stayed for a few days in the house. While I was there, he said, "I remember, you had faith during the war. You had faith. I can't believe the way you had faith." He had come to recognise how faith was being worked out then, even though he was mocking me and tried to test me at the time.

*   *   *   *   *   *   *

After returning to Saint Michel for a few days, the RPF came to us to tell us they had secured the place where Hilary's house was. They were satisfied that there were no Interahamwe still active there and so we went back to Nyamirembo. When we arrived at her house, what we found was just a shell. All the furniture and possessions had gone and the house was completely empty. Even the doors had been removed. Though it was very hard to see their home in that condition, we were still grieving the loss of Bosco and other loved ones. To us all, other things did not matter and Bosco's absence made the house feel empty anyway.

The house girl, Louise, was still living there and she told us about the day we left to go to Gisimba Orphanage. She told us that less than half an hour after I had gone, twenty-seven Interahamwe came into the house and searched every room. They broke down doors and searched everywhere, wanting to find and kill us.

I wondered if they were the same people I saw running away after the bomb had exploded in the market place. Maybe they had been so furious that they had decided to come to search our house to kill us, but we were not there.

I know that the angel of the Lord had been camping around us in Hilary's house, and when we left, so did our angelic protection. Evil was searching for more people to destroy there on that day, but those people had left! *The angel of the Lord encamps around those who fear him, and he delivers them. Taste and see that the Lord is good; blessed are those who take refuge in him (Psalm 34:7-8).*

*   *   *   *   *   *   *

We were able to go outside and sit in the sunshine and move from place to place whenever we wanted. This was what I had missed so much during the days of the genocide and it was so good to have that freedom back.

I visited a neighbour of Hilary's who was a good friend of mine. Even though it was only a few metres walk away, this had been impossible to do when we were in hiding. When Bosco had died she had been watching and she told me what happened. After the soldiers left our compound, Bosco followed and before he had moved very far from our house some Interahamwe came to pick him up. They took him right next to her house where there was a big pit and started insulting him, calling him a cockroach. Then he said to them, "Why do you think I am a cockroach? Probably you are cockroaches because you are doing wrong by killing people. What wrong have I done?"

They said, "Go to that pit!" They pointed their weapons toward the mass grave, motioning him to move.

He said, "I'm not going." My friend could see they wanted to send him there alive and throw a hand grenade in to kill him. He said again, "No, I'm not going there."

One of them ordered another one to shoot him. He fired the gun and shot Bosco. He was then thrown in the pit and they sent a grenade into the pit after him. After this she heard them having a discussion amongst themselves. They said, "Well, why did we kill this guy? Actually, take his wife and the other little cockroach and kill them too." The "other little cockroach" they were referring to was me. Later on that afternoon, she saw them coming back to get us. That was about six o'clock and the same time that Abdul and the army sergeant had come to visit us. So they didn't carry out their plan.

That's how we were protected. To me it seemed God sent these two men just at the right time for us, but it was too late for Bosco. I remembered back to that day and the exchange between the Interahamwe and the army sergeant. They were checking if the sergeant was from the RPF. I heard that at that time the RPF were trying to search everywhere to find survivors and rescue them. Maybe that's why they checked his identity card but when they saw that he was a government soldier it startled them and they just left.

My friend went on to explain how that same night the Interahamwe killed so many people in the neighbourhood. At one point she could see that they wanted to come inside of our building, but because of the high wall surrounding the compound, they just stood at the gate. As they were standing there they had some discussion.

One said, "Go in and kill her."

Another said, "Well, we've actually begun to mess up, because we are just starting to kill our own. We have killed our brother, Bosco, who had a Hutu ID, and even found our own military inside the house earlier on."

She heard their discussion going back and forth. When the group tried to force one of them to go in and kill, he said, "You go, I am not going... If you kill this lady and the other cockroach, who is going to look after our children? Just give these children a chance or you take them yourself."

So they had these confused discussions. For the whole week afterward this is why they decided not to enter our house even though there was a lot of killing going on all around. To me it was as if God had put this confusion among them during those days.

*   *   *   *   *   *   *

There was a time at Hilary's house when I was feeling down because it had been a few days since I had seen anybody I knew from before the genocide. I was desperate to see some people from my church that I used to pray with. Kigali was a close-knit city where people knew each other, especially us born-again believers. The people I sang with in *Chorale La Fraternité* had either been killed or gone into exile. In a way I was alone at that time - I only saw myself in that place. Many of my friends and members of the church had been killed. Many others had already gone into exile to Congo or Kenya or somewhere else. I was unable to go anywhere and if I fled into exile I would probably have been killed. In those days Rwanda was like a desert, a desolate place for me. In a way, everything was completely different, even though it was the same place I had lived for years.

I decided to go out to find some people, but before I went I prayed, *God I am going to go out. Please give me at least two people that I know, Christian born-again people that I know. Please do that, at least two people.*

At that time there were hardly any cars, and no taxis or buses. I had to walk from Hilary's place in Nyamirembo to the city centre about an hour-and-half away. As I was in the middle of the road near the Anglican Episcopal Church, I crossed paths with someone who knew me. As he looked he was shocked and amazed to see me. He exclaimed, "Hey, my sister, you didn't die, they didn't kill you, how Jesus has protected you!"

We gave each other a hug and I said, "I didn't die, Jesus has protected me, as you have said. I was under His mighty hand. His mighty hand has protected me."

This guy's name was Edison. I was amazed that he had called me 'sister'. Back in 1973 he was in secondary school at the Protestant School at Shyogwe near Gitarama. There he was part of a group who organised to kill people from my tribe. The teacher at his school was murdered and although Edison didn't kill him personally, he agreed with the others to kill. Later in the 1980s he became born-again and as a result of his spiritual renewal, went to the wife of the teacher to ask forgiveness for his part in the death of her husband. The teacher's wife lived in Burundi and later on came to a reconciliation conference in Kigali hosted by African Evangelical Enterprise. She gave testimony of how Jesus had reconciled her with her husband's killers through Edison. They had both been through a time of deep repentance and now were true brother and sister in God. She even called him her son, which showed how close they had become because of God's love in them. Edison had been protecting people from the killers in the genocide, so this brought even more joy to my heart.

Meeting Edison that day was deeply significant for me because of the way that I had prayed to meet brothers and sisters in the Lord.

He wasn't my brother by blood or tribe, simply through the blood of Jesus. For that reason we were family.

After we had spent some time talking, I moved on and as we parted he said again, "Oh my sister, how Jesus has protected you!"

From there I went on to the house of another friend nearby to see if they had survived. These friends were from my tribe. When I arrived by the Episcopal Church I saw a small table at the side of the road. This table I recognised as that which used to be in the living room of my friend's house. I thought these people must have been killed, otherwise I would not see their table in the street. I looked over to their house and saw that all of their windows had been smashed, so I didn't go inside.

I continued walking through the Kiyovu district in central Kigali, walking through the avenues and towards the house of some friends called Viviane and John Gakwandi. As I was approaching their gate I heard someone exclaiming, "Look, look, sweet Immaculée, she's still alive!" It was Viviane calling out to me. "Oh Immaculée, come in. How were you protected, how did God protect you? It's amazing to see that you survived!" We hugged each other. The whole family survived, including her husband and four children.

So that day I asked God for two people, but he gave me more than two. Amen!

* * * * * * *

After a while JoJo's son-in-law, Robert, came from Burundi with the keys to her shop. From that time I used to go sometimes to stay at the shop during the day to keep watch.

Robert brought with him a letter for me that JoJo's husband had sent to him from Belgium. JoJo and her husband had been evacuated there at the beginning of the genocide because of their connections in Belgium. In the letter he wrote, "Immaculée, my daughter, God has protected you, your God has really protected you, we couldn't believe it when we saw you on the TV news still alive. He is an amazing God, I can't believe you survived."

I thought to myself: *Me on TV, on the news in Belgium?* Then I remembered how this had happened. It was the time at Saint Michel when I had run to hug Gaspard and the cameraman was there filming us.

Friends and relatives from so many different parts of the world saw me. My friend Jan was in Russia, studying, and she saw me on the TV alive. Some others were in America. Wherever they were, they knew that I was alive; even my family, who were in Congo.

My eldest sister, Lea, who was living in Kinshasa by then, said that when the genocide ended she asked God one thing about me. She said, "God, I know Immaculée is probably not alive because of the genocide. I'm not asking you to show me that she is alive. What I want to know is the true story about how and where she was killed, so we may be able to go and bury her in a proper way. I don't want to stay in confusion. If she is still alive I want to know it also, but that is not the main thing that I ask you because I know so many people were killed. Most of all I want to know the true story."

Two days after she prayed this, she was at home, and my brother was with some friends in the pub having a drink. The TV was switched on and as he looked up, on the screen he saw me alive on the news. He started slapping the table. He became crazy in his behaviour, excited and with tears in his eyes. His friends around him exclaimed, "Eugène, Eugène, are you okay? Are you okay?"

He said, "Yeah, I am okay! I am all right - she didn't die! She didn't die, she didn't die! I saw her on TV - she's still alive, she didn't die!" He immediately ran off to tell my sister. Then at six o'clock, they were all gathered in the living room to watch the news on TV.

Lea said when she saw it she just cried. For her, it was a great testimony of God's faithfulness, because when she prayed she asked without having any idea of how this would happen. But she asked God for the truth of what had happened to me and then soon after she saw it with her own eyes.

God answered my request, too, because when I said: *God you must protect me and everywhere around the world, they will know that you are my God;* indeed it happened. I didn't know that it would happen like that, but God is a big God and He is a God of miracles. He was able to do it and so everywhere they knew I had survived. Glory to His name!

*   *   *   *   *   *   *

Robert came to visit a second time from Burundi and this time he came with Clarice, to whom JoJo was related, and who had also been working with me in the shop. He went to JoJo's house in the prosperous Kimihurura district of Kigali, to see if anybody was occupying it. There was so much chaos and uncertainty in the aftermath of the genocide. It was difficult to know if people had gone into exile or had been killed, or what were the reasons for houses being empty. There were a lot of people coming back into the country after years of exile and they were looking for houses to occupy.

"Immaculée, Jojo's house is empty," he said, "Would you like to go and live there for the time being with Clarice? It would help us to have someone occupying the house."

"It's okay," I said. "We can go there."

Their house was big, with spacious rooms and a lovely garden. The greens of the vegetation and flowers in bloom didn't even hint at the killing that had flooded the nation. Inside the house, many things had been taken and the rooms were bare. There were a few things left in the house though, and we found a fridge and cooker in the kitchen.

Clarice told me how she had escaped the genocide by flying from Rwanda to Burundi by plane together with JoJo and her husband. She didn't have a passport, so she couldn't continue on with them to Belgium. Instead she went to Bukavu in Congo and stayed with JoJo's sister, Patricia. Whilst she was in Bukavu she had a dream in which she saw Jesus. In the dream, Jesus told her that I was still alive. When she found out that I had survived, she remembered her dream and her faith was so encouraged.

During the day I would walk to Jojo's shop in the city centre to look after it and Clarice would stay at home. In those days I saw so many people were very broken. People were very upset about what had happened. One Adventist pastor I knew passed the shop and saw me there. He was amazed to see me there and to know I was still alive. He hugged me with excitement and said, "I can't believe you are alive! God is great! Tell me more about where you hid yourself and how God protected you."

As we were talking he said, "Oh my daughter, this is the day where in scripture it says, those who are pure will stay pure and those who are unclean will remain unclean. Jesus will come soon, but I don't think the Interahamwe will be forgiven for what they have done. They have killed young people and old, even babies. I don't think God can forgive them for all the innocent people they have killed. They will go to hell for sure."

I said to him, "Well, that's not right. If they repent, God can forgive them."

He kept arguing with me that it was not possible because if God is just, loving, kind and caring, then these people deserve hell because of the way they killed innocent and beautiful people.

We kept arguing about this and he left without even saying goodbye. He was angry with me and upset because of what I said to him. He might have thought that I didn't care and had no sympathy for my people that were killed. But I was talking to him about the reality of the Cross, when Jesus said: *Father, forgive them, for they do not know what they are doing (Luke 23:34).* For those who turn to Jesus and repent, he will never turn them away but will graciously forgive. I was talking about the power and mystery of God's love through Jesus' blood shed on the Cross.

*   *   *   *   *   *   *

One day when I was out and Clarice was at home, some young soldiers came to try and talk to her. But not feeling comfortable to let them into the house whilst she was alone, she told them to come back at a time she knew that I would be there. She was suspicious of their agenda. When I arrived, she told me what happened and that they would come back later. When they knocked on the gate, Clarice went to see who it was. There was a way she could look through the gate without them knowing.

She whispered to me, "Come Immaculée, it's them, it's them." She went to open the gate for them and as they stood there we could see one of them had a gun. When they saw me with Clarice they didn't come but instead turned away and ran quickly. We both started laughing loudly at the way they had become afraid and ran off so quickly. It was so funny. The fear of God was in that place during those days. We thought they had a hidden agenda to do something bad to Clarice, but when the fear of God came on them they just ran away!

In the house we used to spend time worshipping God in thanksgiving and praise. One night we were praising God and the power of God was on me. I was singing loudly and jumping in praise to God.

The next day the neighbours told us that they had come to see what was going on. Because of all the noise they thought there were a lot of people in our house. They climbed the wall to look in but saw only me and Clarice. They laughed because they couldn't believe there were only two of us there. The joy of the Lord was with us.

Despite those times of joy, Rwanda after the genocide had also become a strange place. So much of the country had been destroyed or deserted. I used to think that Jesus was coming back very soon, maybe by the end of 1994. There was no church for me to go to; many things did not function; there were no taxis to get about on.

There were times at JoJo's house when I was down and lonely for friends. I cried out to God and I prayed, *My friends have gone. Bring me someone who is like Hope. Where is my hope, where is my hope?* In my mind the hope I cried for was like the character, Hopeful, in the John Bunyan book I had read, *Pilgrim's Progress*. Although being human characteristics, John Bunyan made these into real people in his story. I too wanted real people whom I could share with. I wanted people whom I knew before the genocide, so we could encourage each other and speak hope to one another.

The hope I cried out for, I also read about in 1 Thessalonians 4:13-18. Here it talks about those who have died in Christ and their resurrection at His second coming. The message for those still alive is to encourage each other and not to live like people who have no hope. I wanted people to share this hope with.

The next day a close friend of mine called Valerie came to visit me and left me amazed at God's goodness in answering my cry. Although Valerie was from the tribe that was killing mine, we were very close and our ethnicity didn't matter to us. She used to live with me at JOC, the hostel for young people. During the genocide she went back to her home area, Remera-Rukoma in Gitarama district, which happened to be where the Scripture Union conference had been held before Easter. Because she was Hutu she didn't suffer so much whilst the genocide was going on. Valerie loved to pray and was a wonderful intercessor.

As we started to pray that afternoon, God spoke through her. What amazed me was that she felt God was telling her that she was my hope. This is exactly what I had asked for when I cried out to God! She prayed, "God has heard your cry. This is the person that you were asking for in your prayer. I am bringing her to you. This is your friend and the one you call hopeful."

She also spoke some prophesy that I am seeing fulfilled even up until today. What God spoke to me through her was amazing. Even when some crisis happened later on, I remembered what she said at that time, because God said, "I will fight for you in this situation." Unfortunately she passed away some years later from intestinal cancer. I was really sad when I heard the news.

Another time I went to the Pentecostal church, known as ADPR. I wanted to have prayer and find other people to be with. I felt down, because I had lost virtually everything that I owned. There was a guy there at the church who spoke about how he, too, had lost all his possessions in the genocide and he was feeling hopeless. But then he was reminded about John Bunyan's story *The Pilgrim's Progress* and the part in the book when the character called Christian had lost his things. In his pocket, however, he found a key called Promise. This key opened so many new doors for him and that gave him fresh hope.

When he said this, it really spoke to me and encouraged me. It was as if I went there that day to hear his words. I was reminded about how God is faithful. Many times we don't see how God works, but He is always faithful.

*   *   *   *   *   *   *

After some time my choir, *Chorale La Fraternité,* started meeting again. We met to see who was there, who survived and who was facing hardship as a refugee. It was an answer to prayer that these people had returned back to me. But so much had changed too. My friend, Denise, who sang in the choir, had been killed. She was one of the ones who had planned to go to the Scripture Union centre with me to pray before the genocide, but unfortunately she couldn't make it there. Others from the choir had gone into exile at the end of the genocide and had since returned. One of them, Gerard, had been put in prison. Even though Gerard was a man of prayer and worked honestly as a tailor, when he returned from exile he was betrayed by some ladies he had worked with. They took his sewing machine and accused him falsely of being part of the genocide.

When I heard that he was in prison, my heart went out to him. I was able to find out that he was innocent and had been the victim of injustice.

The walls that divided people's hearts in Rwanda were so big during to those days. Because of all the murder and injustice that the Tutsi had suffered, people were so angry and many were jealous of the Hutu they saw alive. Some used to say things like, "They are still alive with all of their family, and they didn't lose anything. "

Although I loved my own people, I hated the injustice of Gerard being in prison for something he didn't do. My commitment to God's people, *God's tribe*, was greater than any earthly tribe.

I thought about what to do. *Should I keep quiet and ignore Gerard's need for visitors to comfort and encourage him? Was I going to walk under the fear of man and stay away from him? If I did that I would not have to go to the prison to face the thoughts that people might think I had been involved in the genocide because of my visit to a prisoner?* It was not an easy choice to make but I decided to go and visit Gerard.

I bought some sugar and bread went with a friend to the prison to visit him. We had to stand in the queue outside the prison and wait for the prisoners to come out so we could talk to them. The police did not treat us with dignity. They pushed us and I could see in their faces that they were so angry. They asked us why we were there and I imagined they thought I had connection with the Interahamwe during the genocide and now I was coming to visit them. They thought everyone who was in prison was guilty of genocide and could not believe anyone was innocent.

We spotted Gerard from among the crowd of prisoners and went over to greet him. We were so happy to see him and spend some time talking together. We talked to him for no more than 10 minutes and then the prison guards told us to leave. We gave him the food we had bought him and then walked away.

It was a brief but precious time together. As we walked up the hill from the prison toward the market in Kigali I had a strong feeling of shame. Some of my own people who normally wanted to co-operate with me to share their pain were looking at me. They would be thinking about why I had visited those people who had destroyed our own. I discovered more about walking the way Jesus wanted me to. It was not easy or comfortable. However, God knew my heart was clean and in Him my reputation was safe. My concern was to trust God to break the dividing walls in the nation of Rwanda. In Jesus name they have been broken.

After two years, the case of Gerard was heard by the courts. The ladies who betrayed him had escaped to Congo. The government searched for people to give witness at his trial but found no one. Because they could not find anyone, they released him from prison.

EPILOGUE

Later on I found out the identity of the white missionary who came to bring us water. His story, told in his book *I'm Not Leaving*, is a remarkable testimony to self-sacrifice and courage to serve God in the face of danger. During the genocide I thought he was Canadian because that was what people told me, but I found out he is actually American. His name is Carl Wilkens and he had been working for the Adventist Development and Relief Agency in Rwanda for four years when the genocide broke out. He made the decision to stay in Rwanda and leave his wife and three children, who were evacuated on April 17, along with his parents who happened to be in Rwanda with them at the time. Since they are all US citizens they were evacuated under the auspices of the American Embassy in Kigali. Carl's decision to stay was unique. As far as they know Carl was the only US citizen to stay in Rwanda during the genocide. All the other US citizens left - around 250. Carl even had to sign a declaration that he had refused the help of the US government to evacuate him.

Carl had a good relationship with the Rwandan authorities before the genocide started, so when the roadblocks went up and moving around the city became virtually impossible, he was able to get authority to travel around and moved relatively unhindered. He checked on the ADRA workers especially, but came across Gisimba Memorial Orphanage and was moved by compassion to try and get relief to them because there was so much starvation and sickness among the orphans and refugees. He then tried to come regularly to deliver essential supplies of water and food.

The same day that Damas Gisimba had to flee the orphanage because his life was threatened, Carl turned up just at the right time. He stopped the militiamen from attacking us, then found some gendarmes to keep guard and somehow the Interahamwe withdrew. He then went to try and find help through the authorities of Kigali. He had a good relationship with a colonel but when he was at the office of the Governor of Kigali he was informed that the Prime Minister, Jean Kambanda, was visiting and was encouraged to talk to him about the plight of us at Gisimba Memorial Orphanage. They happened to meet in the corridor and Carl introduced himself and explained that he feared a massacre was going to take place at Gisimba. Jean Kambanda consulted with his aides and then gave assurance to Carl that the orphans would be safe. Within a few days the coaches came to us at Gisimba and that's when Major Karangwa supervised our evacuation to Saint Michel.

Carl also negotiated the evacuation of another orphanage, Vaiter Orphanage, to Saint Michel Cathedral. These were in the basement when we arrived at Saint Michel. Marc Vaiter, the manager of the orphanage, was the white man that we had seen at Saint Michel.

I am so grateful to Carl. Without him we would not have had water or food. Without his courage to talk to the authorities, we would not have been evacuated by the major and taken to Saint Michel. I am so happy that he is now doing well back in the US with his family. In June 2011 I had the wonderful opportunity to meet him, his wife and parents in Spokane, Washington. We remembered with gratitude all God had done for us and it was another kind of miracle to meet him in person.

I was also able to find out more about what happened to Damas Gisimba and in December 2009 went to visit him at the orphanage where he was still the manager.

He told me that four days before we were evacuated on July 1, the RTLM radio called him and said that the Ministry of Health wanted to give a donation for the orphans he was caring for. This wasn't true though but rather was a means to lure him away from the orphanage. When he arrived at the radio station he found someone who really wanted to help him though. This man was Philippe Gaillard, the Chief Delegate of the International Red Cross, also a very courageous man who stayed in Rwanda for the duration of the crisis.

Philippe said he could give some food for the children and so Damas went with him to the Red Cross. When they arrived there, Carl Wilkens happened to call on the radio to alert Philippe of the crisis we were going through at the orphanage. He told them the militia were trying to attack and they also wanted to kill Damas, but he didn't know where he was. Philippe told him immediately that Damas was there with him and passed the radio for him to speak to Carl. Carl told him not to go back to the orphanage because they wanted to kill him. Damas couldn't go back to the orphanage but he also realised he couldn't stay at the Red Cross because the man from the radio station was still with them and would have realised something was happening if he stayed.

On the way back, Damas asked to be left at Saint Michel Cathedral. He said he was going to ask the priest there to lend him a car and to ask for provisions for the children. I believe that God gave Damas the wisdom at that time because then he was able to stay at Saint Michel in safety. He hid there because he didn't want the gendarmes and militia to know where he was.

Marc Vaiter, the manager of the other orphanage, was there too at that time. When he saw Damas he became frightened and asked how his children at the orphanage were doing and why he was walking around. Damas told him the whole situation, then Marc called Carl Wilkens on his radio. Carl was relieved to hear that Damas was there safely and told him he was trying to get some gendarmes to guard us at the orphanage but would try to come and see him after that. Around six o'clock Carl arrived at Saint Michel. He said that the authorities had only given him three gendarmes, but having seen him and the gendarmes was enough to make the militia lose courage and withdraw from their attack.

Damas said his time at Saint Michel was not really hard, but there were some soldiers who wanted to take the adults, saying there should only be children staying there. But he was only there a short time. After four days, we joined him following our evacuation and three days after that the city was captured and we were all freed.

*   *   *   *   *   *   *

The hurt and the pain in Rwanda are still enormous, but I love my country and I know God loves all people in Rwanda. To feel the pain that He feels for the people must be unbearable for any person to cope with. There is so much good news coming from Rwanda of people who are reconciled with those who did the killing. It is a great testimony of the power of forgiveness and courage in the face of suffering.

I met the Adventist pastor again after two years. When I saw him he was a totally new person. He said, "My daughter, I'm glad to see you again. That time we met at JoJo's shop, I was very broken and didn't understand God's grace and mercy over all that He has made. I have forgiven them now and I know God will forgive them if they repent."

I have tried to encourage others to forgive. Many times, the first question they would ask would be: "Where were you when the genocide happened?" I told them that I was there and God did protect me.

Some of the RPF soldiers who didn't believe there is a God said, "If we didn't arrive at the right time, God would not save you, because God didn't save the other people."

I said, "Well, I say I survived not because you came, but because God protected me."

It takes time to heal. I don't mind telling about the miracles God did. I have freedom in my heart to do that, but all the other events, I don't like remembering or speaking about. For me healing is not about forgiving these people, because I was even praying for them during the genocide. I remember thinking that many of them were driven by fear, having been coerced by the genocidal government and community leaders. It was not them simply choosing this. They had allowed the forces of darkness to take control of them.

This motivated me to pray for them even more. They used to work in the night, in the rain. They didn't have a chance to sleep; they were just searching for people they didn't know to kill them simply because of their tribe. *These people need God, I thought, I need to pray for them.*

Even to this day, when I dream, sometimes I see friends who were killed. One is a friend called Denise. In my dream, I may say, "Denise, were you not killed? Where have you been since the genocide stopped? I haven't seen you for a long time." In my dream she doesn't approach me. Then I wake up and I realise I have been dreaming. That kind of healing takes time.

With some people who were killed, the circumstances of their death are not clear. With others, we assume they are dead but then we discover they are still alive. So it gets confusing when life and death are blurred like this. We have had some people who were hiding or in the refugee camps. Some had children who were taken by neighbours. Then five years later we see someone who says, "Oh, they have been found. They didn't die, and they weren't killed."

So, just because you haven't seen someone dead or been to their funeral, you think maybe you might see them alive again. You still hold hope, even though they were killed. Your mind can get confused in this way.

*   *   *   *   *   *   *

May the healing in Rwanda continue and may God's love be known to all the people of my nation. Each one is valuable in His eyes.

I am full of gratitude to so many good people who were part of my story of survival and overcoming in 1994. My first thanksgiving goes to the God of the Universe who was able to protect me in the midst of the calamity happening in my country and who brought people He used for my protection. If it wasn't for God who made the way, I would have stayed at JOC hostel and been killed with my roommate Françoise.

With tremendous obedience, Carl Wilkens and his family decided that he should stay in Rwanda, when all other Americans left the country. He chose to obey God's voice and stay even though it might have cost him his life. He didn't walk under fear, but chose to lay down everything he had to serve the Rwandan people. I want to honour his family, especially his wife, who released him to stay. Even though his family loved him, they were able to see the bigger picture of saving people who could not repay him in any way. May the Lord give you the reward on earth and later in heaven.

Thank you to Damas Gisimba. How will I honour you? Only God sees everything, but if the heroes of faith in Rwanda will be written in a book, then I would include you. I thank you for receiving me and all the people who found a hiding place in Gisimba Memorial Centre. I thank you that you did not consider your life, but served so many and gave all you had to them without any discrimination. You loved people without thinking what other people said about them. You fought for justice and you won. You spoke the truth and sent away the darkness at a time when it surrounded us. May God remember all you did. May his mercy, favour and blessings be on you and your family.

What can I say to Bosco? Sometimes I wonder why this happened to you. It seems to be a mystery, why I am alive and you are not. I remember your compassionate heart, receiving people who hid in your home. I miss all of you: relatives and friends who were killed in the genocide. I love you and remember you. May you rest in peace.

*   *   *   *   *   *   *

My hope for Rwanda, which I believe is God's hope and not only my own, is to see Rwandans reconciled and united. We used to a have song on the radio which went: *To others God has given gold and diamonds. For us our gold and diamonds are peace and unity among Rwandans.*

Therefore, if anyone is in Christ, the new creation has come: The old has gone, the new is here! All this is from God, who reconciled us to himself through Christ and gave us the ministry of reconciliation: that God was reconciling the world to himself in Christ, not counting people's sins against them. And he has committed to us the message of reconciliation. We are therefore Christ's Ambassadors, as though God were making His appeal through us. We implore you on Christ's behalf: Be reconciled to God. God made him who had no sin to be sin for us, so that in him we might become the righteousness of God. II Cor 5:17-21

As a Rwandan, my dream is that we won't hold on to divisions from the past. My hope is that we will be reconciled to God and one another; that we will take this message to the nations of Africa and beyond. In Genesis 50: 19-21, Joseph said to his brothers *"Don't be afraid. Am I in the place of God? You intended to harm me, but God intended it for good to accomplish what is now be done, the saving of many lives. So then, don't be afraid. I will provide for you and your children." And he reassured them and spoke kindly to them.*

This is my hope: that we will look forward to the hope that God has for us and that we will speak kindly to one another. Like Joseph, we will say, "What the enemy intended to harm us, God will use for his glory." We will be healed from the wounds of the past. We will receive redemption and be like Christ's Ambassadors. We will live in harmony.

I hope and pray we will reach the goal that God has for us: no more genocide, no more revenge, no more division. The next generation will see their grandparents. The past history will be redeemed into something better. We will walk in our beauty and the design that God has for us. We will be a blessing to the nations.

*   *   *   *   *   *   *

Having been so close to death has made me see how precious life is. Each person is intimately known by God, and each person has a beautiful destiny. In a way it has also made me see how close we are to life. I mean real abundant life, the kind of life Jesus demonstrated to us. The kind of life He promised us. I experience that in part because Jesus said that the Kingdom of Heaven is upon us now. But I know that this is only a taste of what I will experience when this present age comes to an end and the Kingdom of God is established in fullness. Then death, sin and Satan will be defeated once and for all.

For this reason it is my desire that my life and testimony gives hope to the hopeless. No matter how hopeless a situation may seem, I want people to know that there is always hope. They should never give up. I saw that in Rwanda in 1994. Whatever you do, never give up hope. Just as God chose me to inspire others through what He did for me, may He also set you apart to reveal His glory in you and through you. Through all this working together for good, the fragrance of Christ will bring peace to the nations.

PHOTO GALLERY

A rare photo of Immaculée that survived the genocide, she is here (far left) with her sister Jemma (who died in a car crash in Nairobi in 1985), Bona who at that time lived in Kisangani with her husband, and Leah (far right) who lived in Bibwe in Congo.

The Scripture Union Centre where Immaculée spend three days of prayer and fasting for Rwanda from 3-6 April. During her time there God spoke to her that she would see people dying like flies and she heard the audible voice of God saying He would put His word on her mouth for the encouragement of others.

Immaculée (left) together with Mutoni and Hilary in 2009. During the genocide Immaculée visited Hilary the night before the killing started. Mutoni was a new born baby at that time.

Immaculée meets Damas Gisimba in 2009 for the first time since the genocide. Damas still manages the Orphanage. In the National Genocide Memorial in Kigali there is a tribute to the courage he showed during the genocide in protecting over 300 refugees.

Gisimba Memorial Centre Orphanage

Immaculée visits her former home at the hostel, *Jeunesse Ouvrière Catholique.*

Chez JoJo the shop where Immaculée worked in the years leading up to the genocide.

Immaculée revisits *Saint Michel* cathedral and stands outside the cave (or crypt) where she was evacuated to from Gisimba orphanage on 1 July 1994.

Immaculée standing outside Hilary's house: the place where she hid for eight weeks before moving to Gisimba orphanage.

Outside Hilary's house where God did miracles to enable Immaculée to pass the roadblocks to arrive to the safety of Gisimba orphanage on 1 June 1994.

At the wedding of Immaculée's youngest sister Emma (centre) to Johnson in Kigali in 2009. (From left to right: Bona, Johnson, Emma, Immaculée, Lea and Eugène).

Immaculée meets Carl Wilkens and his wife Theresa in Spokane, Washington. June 2011

Chronology of Rwanda relating to the Genocide

1885 The Berlin Conference during the "Scramble for Africa" agrees that Ruanda-Urundi should be a protectorate of Germany.

1894 First known European in Rwanda, a German, Count Gustav Adolph Götzen.

1918 Ruanda-Urundi becomes a UN protectorate governed by Belgium.

1926 Ethnic identity cards introduced by the Belgians.

1933 A census carried out by the Belgian administration. Every Rwandan is issued an identity card stating ethnic identity to be Hutu, Tutsi or Twa.

1945 Status of Belgians colonial rule is transferred from UN protectorate to UN Trust Territory.

1957 PARMEHUTU (Party for the Emancipation of the Hutus) is established

1959 Death of the Tutsi King, Rudahigwa, in mysterious circumstances. Hutus rise up against the Tutsi nobility and kill thousands. Many more flee to Uganda, Tanzania, Burundi and Congo.

1 July 1962 Rwanda gains independence from Belgium. More killing of Tutsis and a further wave of refugees, many to Uganda. Grégoire Kayibanda is declared president and PARMEHUTU comes to power.

1963 Further massacres of Tutsis and more refugees leave the country. Half the Tutsi population is estimated to be living outside of Rwanda by the mid 1960s.

25 December 1964 Immaculée born

1967 Another massacre of Tutsis.

1973 More killing of Tutsi. A coup d'édat by Juvénal Habyariamana.

1979 Immaculée's eldest sister, Lea comes to Rwanda to find her and take her to Zaire (now DR Congo). Immaculée then spends two years living with her biological parents and studying secondary school in Bibwe

October 1990 The RPF invades Rwanda from Uganda. Repelled by government troops with assistance from France and Zaire.

February 1993 The RPF launches a fresh offensive and reach outskirts of Kigali. French forces called to help again.

August 1993 Power-sharing agreement between Rwandan government and RPF signed in Arusha, Tanzania.

6 April 1994 Immaculée comes back from prayer and fasting and then goes to her cousin's house in Nyakabanda in the South West of Kigali. Just after 9:00 pm the President's Plane is shot down as it returns from Tanzania, killing Rwanda's president Juvenal Habyarimana and Burundi's president Cyprien Ntaryamira.

7 April1994 Immaculée cannot leave Hilary's house as Radio Mille Colines instructs everyone to stay inside. Roadblocks appear all over the city. Immaculée's roommate is killed at JOC by Presidential Guards. Prime Minister Agathe Uwilingiyimana murdered. Thousands killed.

8 Apri l 1994 Rwandan Patriotic Front (RPF) launches offensive to end genocide and rescue 600 of its troops trapped in Kigali's parliament buildings.

3 May 1994 Hilary's husband is killed. Interahamwe come back later intending kill Immaculée and Hilary, but get confused when they find a Government Army Sergeant in their living room, visiting with a friend. After that the interahamwe refrain from coming back inside their compound.

22 May 1994 RPF captures the airport and Kanombe military camp causing many government soldiers to be redeployed near to Hilary's house. Towards the end of May a government solider sees Immaculée hiding and threatens to kill her, but then gives her ID card back in a respectful way.

2 June 1994 Immaculée moves from Hilary's house to Gisimba Orphanage. Miraculously a bomb explodes next to the roadblock and she walks through after the militiamen and soldiers had run off.

1 July 1994 All children and adults are evacuated from Gisimba orphanage under the supervision of the Army Major Karangwa and relocated to Saint Michel Cathedral in the Kiyovu district of central Kigali.

4 July 1994 The RPF captures Kigali. Immaculée and Hilary stay at Saint Michel whilst the RPF secure the city.

Further reading

Roméo Dallaire, *Shake Hands with the Devil* (London: Arrow Books, 2003). Firsthand account of the genocide through the eyes of the force commander of the UN mission to Rwanda.

Philip Gourevitch, *We wish to inform you that tomorrow we will be killed with our families: stories from Rwanda* (London: Picador. 2000). This American author and journalist tells the story of the genocide in this book.

Meg Guillebaud, *After the Locusts.* (Oxford: Monarch Books, 2005). Stories of forgiveness and restoration happening in Rwanda.

Callum Henderson, *Beauty From Ashes: Journeys of Recovery From the Rwandan Genocide* (Milton Keynes: Authentic Media, 2007). Shocking stories of suffering and amazing testimony of the healing and transforming power of the Gospel. It also contains the story of how Viviane and John Kakwandi survived. These are the friends that Immaculée met when she asked God to give her two friends to meet.

Fergal Keane, *Season of Blood: A Rwandan Journey* (London: Penguin. 1995). The BBC correspondent who reported from both sides of the conflict in 1994.

Linda Melvern, *A People Betrayed: The Role of The West in Rwanda's Genocide* (London: Zed Books. 2000).

Linda Melvern, *Conspiracy to Murder: The Rwandan Genocide* (Revised edition. London: Verso. 2006). British investigative journalist Linda Melvern has had special access to the United

Nations archives and documentation to produce her two books on the genocide.

Dr. H.H. Osborn, *Fire in the Hills: The Revival with spread from Rwanda* (Highland books. 1991). A detailed account of the revival which originated in Rwanda in the 1930's.

Prunier, Gérard *The Rwanda Crisis: A History of a Genocide* (London: Hurst & Co. 1997). Gérard is a French academic and this book is an authority on the history of the genocide.

Antoine Rutayisire, *Faith Under Fire: Testimonies of Christian Bravery* (African Enterprise, 1995). A collection of remarkable stories of resistance against those who carried out the genocide.

Carl Wilkens, *I'm Not Leaving* (www.ImNotLeavingRwanda.com 2011). The autobiographical account of Carl's experience in Rwanda during the genocide. Many times he delivered food and water to us at Gisimba Orphanage.

The Gisimba Memorial Centre: No Place For Fear – A Tribute to Damas Mutezintare Gisimba. (A Publication of African Rights, April 2003. PO Box 3836, Kigali, Rwanda). A fitting tribute to the courage showed by Damas Gisimba whilst we were hiding in the orphanage.

"A True Humanitarian" A Tribute to Carl Wilkens (A Publication of African Rights – Tribute to Courage Series, Issue 3. 2006, PO Box 3836, Kigali, Rwanda).